THE ETERNAL BUSINESS

THE
Eternal
BUSINESS

How to transition a business for the
employee ownership revolution

CHRIS BUDD

 Harriman House

HARRIMAN HOUSE LTD
3 Viceroy Court
Bedford Road
Petersfield
Hampshire
GU32 3LJ
GREAT BRITAIN
Tel: +44 (0)1730 233870

Email: enquiries@harriman-house.com
Website: www.harriman-house.com

First published in Great Britain in 2018.
Copyright © Chris Budd

Paperback ISBN: 978-0-85719-719-1
eBook ISBN: 978-0-85719-720-7

British Library Cataloguing in Publication Data
A CIP catalogue record for this book can be obtained from the British Library.

 Harriman House

In memory of Geoff Cole, 27th Jan 1962 – 25th June 2018.
One of my 'Without Whom'.

ABOUT THE AUTHOR

Chris Budd is the founder of Ovation Finance, a financial planning company. His focus in financial planning has always been to see money as a tool to improve happiness. As well as advising others on the smarter exit option of employee ownership, he has undertaken the journey himself – having sold Ovation to the Ovation Employee Ownership Trust in 2018.

He is the host of *The Financial Wellbeing Podcast* and author of *The Financial Wellbeing Book* and two novels. He writes regularly in the trade press and speaks at conferences. He is a diploma-qualified business coach.

Chris Budd is married, with two children, and lives in Somerset with too many guitars.

CONTENTS

FOREWORD
BY DEB OXLEY

Employee ownership is not niche: there are businesses of all sizes and shapes in every sector that are now partially or wholly owned by their employees. Employee ownership is not new: the oldest employee-owned businesses were established over 100 years ago. Employee ownership does not rely on benevolence or charity: most employee-owned businesses are for-profit, operating in competitive markets, and their transition involved their owners receiving a fair market value for the sale.

However, it *is* true that employee ownership is not well understood nor sufficiently embedded in the business mainstream. I therefore wholeheartedly welcome this book, not least because I passionately believe that employee ownership can deliver a much-needed answer to at least one of the burning economic challenges facing us today – how to develop a more equal and inclusive economy.

In *The Eternal Business*, Chris Budd offers a guide for how to create a truly sustainable business as part of a succession plan, both through his own journey to employee ownership, as well as the stories of those who he has learned from along the way. I congratulate Chris on his tenacity and commitment in pulling together his journey into a book that can help others do the same.

Of course, every business is different and therefore every journey will be unique, starting from a different base and possibly with a different destination in mind. However, employee ownership is a truly flexible model and therefore has wide appeal to all sorts of businesses, from SMEs to family-owned businesses. The common feature of most of them is the owners' desire to ensure that the business can prosper and thrive beyond their ownership of it – in other words, creating an 'eternal business'.

I am proud that the Employee Ownership Association has been leading the campaign for more employee ownership for almost 40 years. In that time the sector has grown significantly – indeed, since 2012, at a rate of approximately 10% per annum. However, there is still more to do until employee ownership is embedded in the business and political mainstream. When that happens, books like this will no longer be necessary; until then, I welcome every opportunity to share stories and information with business owners, their accountants, lawyers, bankers and other advisers so that over time, every one of them can realise the potential of employee ownership.

In the meantime, anyone wishing to uncover more stories of and advice about employee ownership should visit the Employee Ownership Association website at **www.employeeownership.co.uk**.

Deb Oxley
Chief Executive
Employee Ownership Association

INTRODUCTION

As the founder and owner of a small financial planning practice, Ovation Finance Ltd, I found myself repeatedly being asked the same question by business advisers, accountants and other business owners: "What are you doing to add value to your business?"

For some reason I found this an extremely difficult question to answer. Then, one day, I finally realised why. I wasn't focused on the value of my business because I wasn't focused on *selling* my business.

If I sold Ovation, I would end up with a lump of cash in the bank. I would then find myself sat on the sofa the next day without two things: a sense of purpose and an income.

In order to get an income, I could invest, perhaps in the stock market or in a property. What returns might I get? Four per cent, after tax?

If I invested in a small business, however, I should be able to achieve a much better return. More importantly, I could also get involved. In that way I could get an income *and* get my sense of purpose back.

And if I was going to get involved in a business, it should really be in something I know a little about. Like, maybe, a small financial planning practice…

So why sell in the first place!

I realised that I was proud of the little business I had built up. I liked the clients and employees, and felt a duty towards them. And yet, one day, I would need to release some value from my business.

I needed another way.

In order to enable Ovation to continue without me, I realised I needed to reduce the reliance of the business upon me – I needed to hand over control. I had started this process from the very beginning (it isn't called 'Chris Budd Financial Services' for a reason). Now, however, I needed to take this to its ultimate conclusion.

This meant not only making my vision for the business crystal clear, but also embedding that vision into everything the company did. It meant empowering employees to make decisions (as opposed to my previous management style, which tended to be empowerment by not getting involved!). It meant giving the employees a real sense that they were involved with the business – that they had a genuine voice. It meant making Ovation a 'proper' business and not a consultancy based around me.

This process took many years. There was still one piece of the jigsaw missing, however. Having gone a long way to making myself the least important person in the business, I still needed an ownership model that allowed me to extract value (my drawings from the business were often modest, especially in the early years, and I needed to 'catch up'). I did not, however, want to sell the company to a group of employees, nor to a third party, either of whom might just sell on in a few years' time. I wanted Ovation to last forever.

I eventually found the answer in indirect ownership – commonly known as 'employee ownership'. The combination of this ownership structure, plus the changes I had been making in three particular areas, finally gave me what I was looking for.

It is these three areas, combined with the ownership structure, which make up what I refer to as the **eternal pyramid**, the four parts of a business that need to be in place to create a business which has a chance of lasting forever – of becoming an eternal business.

SHOULD YOU READ THIS BOOK?

This book provides a model to enable business owners to release value from their business without having to sell the business to another company.

It provides a model for how business owners can release value from their business without having to sell the business to a leadership team who are forced to take on debt, and then have the problem of how to release value themselves.

It provides a model for employees to contribute to, and benefit from, the business.

It provides steps to follow which will enable a business to enjoy succession beyond its current owners and give it a chance to last forever.

It provides a process by which control is devolved from the few to the many.

It explains how employee ownership works.

It provides a model to build a sustainable business – an eternal business.

If you are a business owner, you should read this book if you'd like to find a new and more effective way to do succession – and a new ownership structure that will enable you to hand over control. You might then give this book to your employees, who can use it to instigate those changes.

A business model for all businesses

The eternal business model involves making a business 'employee-owned'. As well as explaining what that means, this book provides a path to get there and steps to take to give that employee-owned business the best chance of surviving.

However, as the eternal business model centres around making a business no longer reliant on one or a few people, it should strengthen *any* business. (You can't sell a business that still needs you.) Therefore, while *The Eternal Business* proposes employee ownership, other approaches – including partial employee ownership, management buyouts and outright sale – should all be strengthened by following this model. Indeed the outcome of following this path might be selling completely, or selling control but retaining a shareholding for ongoing income.

Employee ownership models around the world

For many years now, employees in the UK have been able to hold a stake in the businesses for which they work. Employee ownership, however, only really took off following *The Nuttall Review of Employee Ownership* in 2012. This led to the creation of the employee ownership trust (EOT), which is designed to give employees not only financial returns but a genuine say in the running of the business. As Graeme Nuttall OBE, author of the *Nuttall Review* and architect of the EOT, says: "an employee share scheme that only delivers financial benefit does NOT create an employee-owned business". The EOT also carries certain tax advantages to encourage companies to become indirectly owned and employee-controlled. The UK is now leading the world in true employee ownership.

When making my own business employee-owned, I chose to do so through the EOT. Although other countries have yet to follow this lead, *there is nothing to stop any company in any country from becoming indirectly owned and employee-controlled.* What is more, other countries are becoming increasingly aware of this innovative model, and international equivalents of the EOT may not be far off.

In the US, the Employee Stock Ownership Plan (ESOP) model – which provides a financial return for the performance of the business – is common. Employees do have votes – however, in the words of Graeme Nuttall, "[t]he employee voice is sometimes not as strong as it might be." A few US companies have recently adopted the UK-style employee trust model, which is building real momentum. However, the tax breaks for ESOP make this the preferred vehicle for many owners, despite the drawbacks.

In Australia, there have been recent major tax law changes to boost employee share ownership in start-ups but more needs to happen to promote employee ownership. The subject has been the subject of hearings in parliament, although, like the US, there is no formal government equivalent of the EOT as yet.

Finally, in Europe, a major report for the European Commission in 2014 included UK case studies, highlighted the UK's unique trust model of 'perpetual EO' and held up the effect of the *Nuttall Review* and the UK Government's support for employee ownership as an exemplar for all of Europe to follow. However, there is still no legal structure common across the European Union.

A WORD ABOUT THE BUSINESS STORIES

The book is peppered with real-life business stories. Most of us like to know that something we are contemplating has already happened to someone before – be it good or bad!

Some of the subjects of the stories have had their names changed at the request of those involved; some have had enough details changed to make them unrecognisable, where the details are sensitive. All these stories, however, are based on real people and events.

HOW TO USE THIS BOOK

This book is not linear. It is not essential to start at the beginning and read through to the end. You can go straight to the section that interests you most; read from start to finish; or flick through, only reading the anecdotes. It may be, for example, that a business owner goes straight to the section on the ownership structure, then hands the book to employees to implement.

BUT: a word of warning. Many owners and advisers get hung up on the tax and legal aspects of employee ownership. What this is really about, however, is building sustainable businesses.

Chris Budd
Somerset, 2018

Chapter 1

WHY ETERNAL?

INTRODUCTION

Being the owner of a small business can be lonely. Nobody really understands the pressures you are under. Everyone's problems are yours, but your problems are your own. You have invested time, money and reputation into the business, and it can be hard to see a way out that both gives you a financial return and continues the work you have started.

Being an employee of a small business also brings its own challenges. You can talk directly to the boss, but they don't always listen. You don't really know how well the business is doing. You'd like to share in any success of the business, but may not have any money to buy in (if that is even an option). The business would be so much stronger if only you and your colleagues could make a few changes, but the boss is set in their ways.

The model of the eternal business provides answers to both these sets of problems.

The intention of this book is to provide an alternative to traditional business succession models – to provide a pathway for handing over control of a business. The owner[1] might sell and then exit completely,

---

[1] Or owners. But to avoid cluttering the text with brackets or 'and/or', I will generally refer to owner in the singular throughout. The book applies equally to businesses with multiple owners.

or might affect a partial sale, retaining a minority shareholding and perhaps a role in the business.

We will set the scene by looking at the issues business owners face when considering the succession of their business, and the typical solutions offered to them. We will look at the challenges faced by a fictional business owner, Mike Procter, as he tries to release value from the business he spent so many years building. We will consider the typical path Mike would go down, then see how making his business eternal may be the best way to achieve all his objectives.

We then finish with a short section which touches on why the eternal business model is also hugely beneficial for employees (although chapter 7 looks at life in an eternal business from the employee's perspective in greater detail).

Since the initial decision to become employee-owned will come from the existing owner, the majority of this chapter is therefore aimed at the business owner. Given that any decisions around succession also affect those working for the business, however, it will also be of interest to employees.

Again, it is worth noting that although the book is not aimed at business owners who want to sell to the highest bidder, it is true to say that getting a business ready to be taken over by the employees is also likely to make it more attractive to a buyer.

WHY DO PEOPLE SET UP THEIR OWN BUSINESSES?

Owning and building a business requires great sacrifices in terms of time, money and energy. There must surely be something sitting on the other side of the scales to balance out the experience; to make it worthwhile.

As we'll see later, the reasons people set up their own businesses invariably centre around personal satisfaction. It might be creating a great team of people; having a positive social impact; perhaps inventing something that solves a problem (often one that they might have suffered from personally). Some talk of having a sense of purpose. The words 'respect' and 'challenge' often appear, as does 'independence'.

Interestingly, money does come up, but it's rarely the first thing mentioned, or even the second or third. When it does get mentioned, it is usually in terms of financial security, either in retirement or for the family.

What do you *want* from your business?

Given that respect and pride feature so highly in building a business, surely exiting a business should reflect these priorities?

Perhaps we need a way to exit a business that will ensure that the company continues – that a cherished business which has been painstakingly built up over many years will continue to do the good thing it was set up to do.

Now, this won't be attractive to everyone. For some, maximising wealth is the key. For others selling to a much larger business is the only way to achieve personal goals. This book will still be of interest to such people, as many aspects that make a business eternal will also help to make it more saleable.

The Eternal Business will, however, be of greatest interest to the owner who is proud of their business: proud of what they produce, proud of the team of people, proud to be called the founder.

It will be of particular interest to such a person who cannot see how they can have their cake and eat it – how they can exit (or partially exit) their business and yet leave it to people who will carry on the good work. And how they can extract value without placing employees in debt or creating a culture of 'haves' and 'have-nots', with some staff able to afford to buy shares and others not.

How, in other words, they can exit their business in a truly successful way.

What do you *need* from your business?

To answer the question of what makes a successful business we first need to provide a definition of success.

This tends to vary greatly. For some a definition of a successful business is one that hasn't gone bust yet. Yet even a business that has gone bust after 20 years could be deemed successful if it kept people employed for two decades, put the kids through school and repaid the mortgage.

Many will define success by how they are viewed by their peers. This will often be an amount of money – although where that figure comes from is usually somewhat arbitrary. My personal definition of success is 'flexibility of time'.

Valuation rivalry

Angie told me that she needed to sell her business for £1m. I observed that this was a very round figure, and asked where this figure had come from. She talked in vague terms about market valuation and what her accountant had told her it was worth.

I pressed Angie on this valuation, asked her if she had anything in writing. After ten minutes or so, she admitted that her sister had sold her business for £1m, and she wanted to sell her business for at least as much as her sister.

Having provided financial planning and advice to many business owners over the years, I have often noticed that the answers to the questions "How much do I need?" and "How much is my business worth?" tend to be rather similar. If 'someone' values your business at a certain level, then that is the value of your business – and the amount you simply must have for the life you want.

Often people take their benchmark of financial success from their peers. The trouble is, the amount that someone else tells you they sold their business for bears no relation to what your business might be worth (there's also a fair chance it bears no relation to how much they ended up getting, but that's another story!).

How does one value a small business? It is something of a cliché that a small business is only worth what someone wants to pay for it. Indeed, a corporate financier friend of mine once told me that "most businesses fail to sell, and the most common reason is vendor expectation."

Perhaps 'How much is my business worth' is the wrong question. How about instead we ask 'How much do I *need* my business to be worth?'

Selling for the wrong objective

Many years ago a client told me she was depressed and stressed. Rachel was 61, she had been running her business for some 20 years and just wanted to get out. In her words, she was feeling desperate.

Her accountant had given her a letter advising that, in his opinion, the business was valued at £1.5m. During a financial planning meeting, Rachel said that she and her husband planned to retire to the house in Spain that they owned, selling their UK property. I advised that the funds this would generate, plus their sizeable pension fund, would be enough for them to live on. Anything from the sale of the business was a nice bonus, but probably wouldn't affect how they lived in retirement.

The client's accountant made some enquiries, and came back with two offers, both for less than £1m. I spoke with Rachel, who said she had turned down the offers. When I asked why, she said because she had worked hard on her business for many years and wasn't just going to give it away to someone.

I reminded Rachel that her primary objective was to get rid of the business; also that they didn't actually need the money. She repeated that the business was worth £1.5m, so why would she sell it for less?

I commented that it was only the accountant who said the business was worth £1.5m, and that the two offers would suggest otherwise. Furthermore, the value is irrelevant when the main objective is to move on. Rachel brought the conversation to a close, insisting that she wanted full value for the business and anyway had already rejected the two offers.

Rachel eventually sold the business eighteen months later for £1.2m. She and her husband retired to Spain. Six months later I heard that she had suffered from a nervous breakdown.

Being pulled not pushed

The very first step to deciding on the future of your business is therefore answering the question of how much you need to get from the sale of the business – and that means planning your future.

The question of what you need your business to be worth can only be answered by considering what life might look like beyond the business, and what this might cost. Many owners have given no thought to what they will do once the business is sold. They have been so busy working *in* the business that they have not looked up for many years – not only have they not worked *on* the business, they have not spent time thinking about their own needs.

Having something to go to after the business has been sold is possibly one of the most important steps the owner can take. We'll touch on this again later, but being pulled away from the business and into another area is far more likely to result in a successful succession than if the owner is being pushed into the process.

The starting point for the business owner, therefore, should be to get clarity over what the future might hold, and what the business needs to provide for them. This planning should involve creating objectives and motivations, then creating a financial plan to get there – a clear path to identifiable objectives.

As with so much of the journey to an eternal business, it's a good idea to get help, and creating a financial plan is no exception. My previous book, *The Financial Wellbeing Book*, provides the steps to take to create a plan to make you happier not just wealthier. Even better, engage a financial adviser to help you work through the process (tip: if you do use a financial adviser, make sure you use one who does planning, with cash flow forecasting, and preferably who has been trained in using coaching skills).

In this way a business owner can answer the question of what the business *needs* to be worth.

THE STORY OF PROCTER AND GRACE LTD

Let us start this examination of *how* to construct a business that will last forever by looking at *why* an owner would choose such a path in the first place. We'll do this by considering the life of a fictional business: Procter and Grace Ltd.

Michael Procter and Bill Grace set up their consultancy business because they had a passionate belief that current ways of providing advice in their sector were flawed. They not only saw a gap in the market, they had a vision for a way of delivering significantly better outcomes for clients – as well as being profitable. This proposition would result in long-term clients and therefore create a business with value. At least, that was the plan!

The exit from Procter and Grace Ltd - version 1

Twenty years later, and Mike is still running the business. They nearly went bust in the first few years and Bill, uncomfortable with the risk, sold his shares to Mike, who was the real visionary of the two. Mike continued to work hard and slowly but surely built a business based around a clear set of principles. The business defined him just as much as he defined the business.

Financially, Mike had still not caught up with where he would have been had he carried on in an employed position. He had a modest pension fund, was still paying off a mortgage on the house and had minimal savings. He did, however, have a company that he was extremely proud of, with a track record of strong profits and loyal clients.

Mike received offers to buy his business. Several were disappointingly low but one offer, from a medium-sized regional firm, matched his expectations. He accepted the offer and, after an extremely stressful few months, the first payment landed in his account and he handed over the keys to the office. Future payments would depend upon the new company retaining clients, although he had little say in the ongoing service they were offering.

Mike and his wife went travelling for a month, including the tour around South America that they had always promised themselves. When they got back, Mike played more golf. He kept in touch with some of his old employees, who he considered to be friends, and met them for lunch once a month. He heard that the new owners were making some changes, not all of which he approved of. Still, it wasn't his business any more, he had handed over control to the new owners.

A year later, and the second payment came in, only it wasn't as big as had originally been anticipated, because not all the clients had stuck around. The feedback from his old colleagues was that the business wasn't like it used to be. Some of them had handed in their notice and were moving on. The company that Mike had built up and was so proud of was not the same any more.

The third payment was considerably smaller than the second payment. Bored with golf and keen to increase the income from his investments, Mike bought shares in a local business, and took a directorial position.

Four years after the sale of his business, Mike heard that it had been sold on, this time to a large corporate who merged the clients into its own business. Proctor and Grace Ltd was no more.

The exit from Procter and Grace Ltd – version 2

Mike sold his business because, well, that's what you do, isn't it? For years people had been asking Mike what his business was worth, and what was he doing to add value to his business. All his fellow business owners talked about was selling their business one day.

Let's rewind that story. Let's go back to the point at which Mike received the offer to buy his business. Let's now take Mike down a different future.

Instead of accepting the offer, Mike did two things. Firstly he took some financial planning advice, in order to work out how much he *needed* to sell the business for.

In doing this financial planning he quickly realised that in order to financially forecast his future, he would need to work out what it was he actually wanted to do once the business was sold. What did he want his future to look like? This was not something he'd thought much about before.

Mike's financial plan

The financial planning took the form of a cash flow forecast, which provided a numerical picture of their financial future. Mike had been so busy running his business that he had not previously thought beyond a possible future sale. Now Mike and his wife, Charlotte, were forced to think seriously about what they wanted their future to look like. They took a few guesses, made a few assumptions, and pressed the button.

The first thing that Mike and Charlotte realised that they needed was *income*, not just capital. Sure, they would like to pay off the mortgage and buy a new car, but what they really needed was an income for life.

That income, however, needed to last forever, long after Mike was no longer actively involved in the business. Rather than getting the business ready to be sold to a third party, therefore, Mike needed to get it into a state where it would survive – and thrive – without him.

Suddenly the future looked different.

What Mike loved about his business

Mike spent a few sessions with a business coach. Halfway through the second session, the coach asked if she might make an observation. She commented that Mike only became really animated and engaged when discussing one of three subjects. They were: his family; cycling; his business.

This led to further discussion, and Mike began to realise two things about his business. Firstly, that he was very proud of it and didn't actually want to see it disappear into a larger organisation. Secondly, that he cared deeply about his staff and clients, and was worried about what might happen to them after the sale of the business.

A happy business

Business owners are often people who care about their clients and their employees. Whether they founded the company or took it over, the drive and energy needed to run a successful business means that they often do not want to see that business sold to someone who will rip the company apart.

Faced with the reality of selling his business, Mike Procter realised that he had established the company on a set of principles. He didn't want to see those principles sold along with the business. He didn't want the staff to lose their jobs, or the clients to receive a service inferior to the one he had been so proud of over the years.

These were people whose respect mattered to him and who, frankly, he had to look in the eye after the sale.

Previously Mike had thought that the large corporate offer was the only one that matched his own valuation of his business. With the financial planning behind him, however, he realised that although he did need to receive some money, his requirement from selling the business was not simply to maximise the valuation.

Mike concluded that he had several specific objectives when considering the future of his business:

- he DID NOT want the business to be sold to a third party who didn't understand it

- he DID want the business to continue his vision for making happy customers

- he DID want the company to provide its employees with financial security

- he DID want the company to continue to be a happy place to work.

In addition there were his personal objectives from the financial planning:

- to release some capital

- the option of an ongoing income

- the option of an ongoing role, at least in the medium term (a sense of purpose).

Mike spoke to his various business advisers in an attempt to find a succession plan that might fulfil the needs of himself *and* the customers *and* the employees.

If selling to a third party was not an option for him, Mike was told by his advisers that the only other option was to sell to his employees.

The management buyout

In order to achieve some of Mike's business objectives, one route might be that some of the employees get together and buy some or all of his shares, thereby taking over control of the business. This is known as a management buyout, and can take various forms. Note that the term 'management' in this context really means anyone who wants to join in buying the business.

Although they can be very successful, management buyouts are fraught with difficulty. There are a number of reasons why this route can go wrong:

> If the shares were simply given to employees, this is likely to be treated as income and would create a tax liability on the employee. It is generally not a viable option.

In order to buy shares, however, employees need to have the money to do so.

Not everyone has sufficient savings or is able to raise a loan.

The ones that do have the money might not be the most talented ones.

Management buyouts are therefore often funded by loans. This creates pressure on the leadership team that they will not have experienced before. Are the employees prepared to take on this risk? Does the owner want to put their employees in such a position?

There is a big difference between being an employee and an owner. There are many reasons leadership teams do not work as effectively as the owner they have bought out, including:
- lack of clear leadership within the team
- not having a sufficiently robust shared vision of the future of the business
- different personal objectives.

And finally, how do the new owners, the leadership team, realise their value?

According to The Turnaround Management Society, when asked for the most common internal causes of a corporate crisis, 51% of business turnaround specialists surveyed replied: "The management had no vision." Other management failings came in second and third.

In the excitement of becoming a business owner via a buyout, this last point can often be overlooked. In selling shares to employees, the owner is not solving the problem – they are passing on their problem to someone else. When it comes time for the new owners to sell, they need to have someone with the available money to buy *their* shares.

When you can't retire because you can't sell your shares

Handsome Brittle and Splodge Property Consultants is a company made up of eight directors and 55 employees. Directors own the shares in the business, initially acquired through a management buyout from the founders 20 years previously. Selected employees have subsequently been promoted to director and been given the opportunity to buy shares from departing directors.

A smaller pot of shares has been set aside, and employees are invited to buy shares of retiring directors, creating an 'internal market' for the company.

At the time of writing, two of the directors are unable to retire because there is no one in the business willing or able to buy their shares from them.

The assumption of the sale

Mike discussed his succession plans with his business advisers. They all assumed that it would be some form of management buyout, whereby some of his employees would buy some of Mike's shares. They all raised difficult questions:

- Will you retain a controlling interest?

- Do you wish to retain a shareholding in case the company is sold one day?

- How will you get the shares back if someone leaves?

- Are the ones who can afford to buy the business the ones you would choose to look after the business?

- What happens if you have minority shareholders that you no longer want to be part of the business?

- How will the leadership team sell their shares and realise their value? Will this be a trade sale?

Mike came to realise that the language around business ownership is entirely centred on one central premise: one day the business is going to be sold. He wanted to find a different approach, one that took the focus away from the value of the business. After all, if the business was never going to be sold, why did the value matter?

An approach was needed that would allow Mike to extract himself from the company and achieve his personal objectives, that would leave the company in the control of the employees – yet did not involve selling the shares to the employees.

How much is enough?

Mike's financial planning enabled him and Charlotte to work out what they needed for a happy life – their 'how much is enough?' figure.

They realised that although they needed some capital, they didn't need the entire value of the business as long as they continued to receive some ongoing income.

Once they received what they needed for their happy life, any extra profits would be available to give to the employees. So if they could only sell the majority of shares to the employees somehow, they could retain a small shareholding for income.

Sounds generous? It isn't.

If the majority of the profits were made available to the employees, they would be incentivised to keep the business running efficiently, and generating the profits which would pay the income that Mike and Charlotte needed.

The plan started to form

Finally, Mike realised what it was that he wanted to do. In order to realise all of his objectives, both personal and business, he would sell the majority of the company but retain a minority interest from which he would receive an income.

There were, however, two main flaws in this plan:

- To whom would he sell the business, if not a third party nor the employees?

- The financial future for Mike and Charlotte would be dependent upon being paid from a business over which they no longer had control.

The answer seemed to be for the company to be owned *indirectly* – in such a way that it would last in perpetuity. Mike needed to make his business eternal.

FOR THE EMPLOYEE

As we will see, an eternal business is one that focuses not on value, but on long-term sustainable profit. For a business to be eternal, it needs employees who will want to work there for the long term. This will be achieved by the employees benefiting from the success of the business, and having some control within the business – being given the opportunity to make a real difference.

For employees to understand how different life will be in an eternal business, we need to go through the different aspects of what such a business looks like.

In chapter 5 we will look at what makes meaningful employment. To ease us in, let's take a brief look at what happened to one of the employees of Procter and Grace.

Zaheer had worked for Procter and Grace for five years. He joined the company because he had met Mike at a conference and he found that their principles were aligned. He had become frustrated, however, as he found that Mike wasn't listening to his ideas. He began to find himself complaining to his partner about Mike, wishing he would let others 'inside' the business, to allow Zaheer to have a say. He had so many good ideas, but no one in the business to tell them to.

Although Zaheer continued to feel passionate about what the company did, he just didn't feel engaged.

Adding to this growing sense of frustration was the fact that he did not know what Mike planned for the business long term. Although he was well rewarded financially for his job, Zaheer had the nagging doubt that all he was really doing was helping to build the business so that Mike would sell it. There had been some talk in the pub after work with some of his colleagues that Mike might let them buy the company from them, but Zaheer didn't have any money. Besides which, the more successful they made the company now, the more they were going to have to find to buy Mike's shares in a few year's time.

Although Zaheer loved his job, he was beginning to wonder if he might need to look elsewhere, to work for a company that would really give him what he wanted. Real satisfaction, not only of his job, but somewhere that he could really feel valued and involved, *and* share in the financial success of the business. Now that would be a company he could see himself working in for the rest of his life…

CONCLUSION

At the start of this chapter, we asked what is meant by an 'eternal business', and why someone would choose such a structure.

The notion of making a business eternal involves changing the focus away from increasing value. It means shifting the ultimate goal from selling a business to building one that can last forever.

Once the objective of selling for a capital gain is removed, the approach to the business changes. The focus moves to long-term sustainable profit instead of increasing sale value – and that means happy staff and happy clients.

This is attractive for employees because they have increased meaning in their roles as they get to contribute towards business decisions and influence their own destiny. They also benefit from the success of the business without the need to risk their own money.

This is also an attractive proposition for a business owner. It provides a way to exit the business without compromising the principles upon which it was founded. They can sell the business and receive the proceeds over time from future profits. They may also choose to retain a minority shareholding to provide an income.

This does, however, mean that the financial security of the owner will be reliant upon a business that they no longer control.

This sentence is **the** key driver for the existence of this book. In order to reduce the riskiness of the source of the payments, the structure of the business must have certain features. These can be categorised into four sections; the four sides which make up the eternal pyramid.

Chapter 2

THE ETERNAL PYRAMID

INTRODUCTION

T he structure and organisation of a business that aims to last forever will be very different to a business that, for example, is being prepared to be sold to a third party.

We are looking to build a business that will leave a legacy; that will provide employment and fulfilment for many years to come; that will thrive and prosper long after the owner has departed. We are concerned with making that business eternal, and to achieve this we must make the business not reliant on any one individual.

The eternal pyramid provides a model to motivate employees and engage them in the ongoing success of the business, thereby achieving this aim. Constructing it also provides a steady process for the control of the business to move safely from one or a few people to the employees.

The eternal pyramid is formed of the four key areas that will help to reduce the likelihood of a business failing. As a pyramid it is a structure in which all four sides lean on – and thereby support – each other.

REDUCING THE RISKINESS OF THE BUSINESS

Many business owners who sell their businesses to their employees face a particular challenge. Whether they sell to a leadership team, to a new holding company, or to an employee ownership trust (see chapter 6), most succession plans involve the exiting owner being paid from future profits of the business.

Most people who have started a business will have made financial sacrifices along the way. Their financial future is often dependent upon the sale of the business – hence the oft-used phrase 'My business is my pension'.

When it comes to selling the business, therefore, the owner's financial security comes from future profits of a business which they no longer control.

That can be a pretty scary prospect!

One of the objectives of the eternal business, therefore, is to reduce the riskiness of the business. For the business owner, this may well feel like the *only* objective!

But wait – reducing the riskiness of a business? That's not what entrepreneurs *do*, is it?

SWIMMING AGAINST THE TIDE

An entrepreneur is someone who invests in, and helps build and sell, businesses.

A small business owner is often someone who started doing something they enjoyed doing, then one day realised that they were now running a business and no longer doing the thing they enjoyed doing.

The image of the entrepreneur is often someone who takes risks and gets rewarded grandly for doing so. Films such as *The Wolf of Wall Street*, programmes such as *Dragons' Den*, all combine to make owning and controlling a business seem sexy and exciting.

In practice, most businesses don't get films made about them. Most businesses are either exciting and fail, or rather dull and moderately successful. Almost by definition, an eternal business will be one that is a little more cautious in nature.

The eternal business model is not for serial entrepreneurs; City investors; corporate financiers; venture capitalists. This model is aimed at the business owner and employee who want a business that is enduring and sustainable. The perfect eternal business is one that is taking only as much risk as is required to achieve the personal objectives of the owners and the employees (which, as we will see, are actually very similar).

Finding your priority

Five years after starting Ovation I finally began to feel that it might be around for the long term. At the time my wife and I had two very young children.

I sat down with my wife one night and asked for her guidance. I explained that I felt I had two choices with the business, now that it had reached a degree of security.

The first option, I explained, would be for me to work hard. I could work until 7pm each night, get back in time to tuck the kids into bed, and work some

Saturdays too. I felt that if I worked such hours there was a good chance I could build a business with serious value. We could, at some point in the future, end up pretty wealthy.

Option two, I went on, would be for me to work fewer hours. Be home in time for tea with the kids and to read them a story, and to make it a rule not to go into the office on weekends. This way I still felt I could build a profitable business, but it would be one that would make us comfortable, not wealthy.

I was willing to follow either path, and I left it up to my wife to decide which it would be. Without thinking for more than five seconds, she chose to have a life that we would have the best chance of enjoying. She chose option two.

HOW TO MAKE A BUSINESS ETERNAL

In order to allow the existing owner to hand over control, a business will need to display a number of features:

- good quality business decisions, aligned to a vision
- not reliant upon one or a small number of individuals to provide the vision
- not reliant upon one or a small number of individuals to make the decisions
- employees who are truly motivated and inspired by their jobs
- employees who are rewarded for the success of the business.

These are in addition to the usual elements of good business practice common to any business, such as having clear workflows and procedures.

Reducing the riskiness of a business to a level that allows the owner to entrust their future income to others requires commitment at all levels. This is not a plan that can be entered into half-heartedly. It also takes time.

The four parts of an eternal business

The actions needed to make a business eternal can be broken down into four areas:

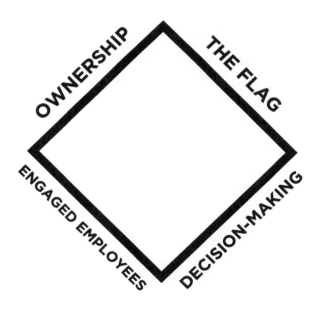

- **The flag** refers to the flag in the ground around which we all gather; the flag at the head of the parade which the marching band follows; the sense of purpose of the business. It also means everything which happens that helps to align the business to this purpose. Marketing; branding; service proposition and/or product design; recruitment; workflows.

- Collaborative **decision-making** within an eternal business will engage all employees and reduce the impact of one or a few people leaving.

- In order to be happy and motivated in their roles, a clear financial and career plan will result in **engaged employees**.

- For a business to be eternal, the **ownership**, and therefore both control and future profit, needs to be shared in order to motivate and inspire the employees. An eternal business will be indirectly owned in favour of the employees, and employee-controlled.

The eternal pyramid

Although improving these four areas will aid any business, for a business to move towards being eternal, *all* of these areas need to have been strengthened. Furthermore, they need to have been worked on concurrently.

For example, the decision-making procedures must be mapped against a clear sense of purpose for the business (the flag). Both these areas of the business need to be improved together in order to inform each other's progress.

Similarly, the business needs a clear sense of how being an employee can help them achieve their life objectives (engaged employees). It will therefore needs an ownership structure which shares the rewards of the business with the employees.

Furthermore, having good collaborative decision-making structures will improve employee engagement.

We can therefore see that the four key elements that make a business eternal are not actually a square; they form a pyramid, each side leaning against the others.

They form the **eternal pyramid**:

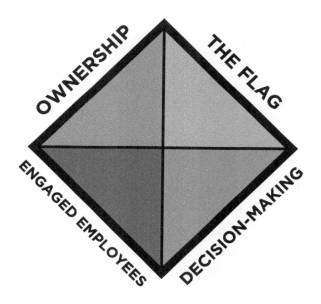

This principle of a pyramid runs through the eternal business model. Four areas of the business, each leaning on the others; each being worked on at the same time as the others; lessons learned from one side being used to improve the construction of another side.

Decide first, action last, prepare in between

A key principle of the process of handing over control is that once the decision is taken, there is a lot of work to do before the final change in ownership takes place.

The ownership side of the pyramid involves the employees of the business taking control from the owner. This requires building the pyramid slowly, all sides being erected at a similar pace. For example, the owner learns to let go, while at the same time the employees start thinking more like business owners. Both processes take time and inform each other.

A change to one side of the pyramid can have a significant impact on developments in another area. Engaging employees in the running of the business does not happen overnight. It involves the building of trust – on both sides.

Building trust, engaging employees

The single biggest step change in Nevil Ltd successfully moving to employee ownership was when the (sole) owner of the business sat down with the employees and talked them through the accounts of the business.

Previously he had been nervous of sharing what he felt was sensitive financial information about the business. When the meeting came, he was prepared to defend his own drawings based on the risk he had taken in setting up the business in the first place. He was expecting to point out that the staff bonus came before he took the remaining profits.

When the employees were talked through the accounts, the subject of the owner's drawings didn't even come up. Instead, there was great surprise at the strength of the balance sheet. One employee commented that he had always assumed the business was one bad month away from going bust, and had no idea of the reserves that the owner had set aside.

The overall reaction was hugely positive that the company had been run so well financially, and a far greater understanding of how the business worked had been reached. As a result, employee engagement in collaborative decision-making became much more positive.

Drawing on the experience of firms who have transitioned to employee ownership, several common threads have emerged:

- problems could have been more easily dealt with if raised *before* making the formal change to the ownership of the company

- many of the issues would have been prevented or even solved through better information flow; in particular, there is often a lack of explanation given to employees as to what the differences are going to be once the company is employee-owned

- a lack of clarity over the ongoing role of the owner prevented the employees from stepping forward.

Transitioning from a traditional small business structure, where a few people make business decisions and the rest of the employees act to a greater or lesser degree in their own self-interest, does not happen overnight. And the advantages of aligning interests takes time to permeate through.

Information flow and shared purpose

The 'prisoner's dilemma' is a psychological paradox which demonstrates how two people acting logically and in their own self-interest can create a worse outcome than if they had cooperated.

Suppose two criminals are arrested for a robbery. They are facing one year in prison if they do not say anything at all. Each is offered the same deal. If you betray the other, your sentence will be two years. If you remain silent and the other betrays you, you will get three years. Logically, therefore, both should remain silent and get one year.

However, self-interest kicks in – and means they are more likely to betray the other rather than stay silent while the other might betray them. As they both end up betraying each other, they each get two years. Acting in self-interest has created a worse outcome for them both.

How can the prisoner's dilemma be avoided? If the two prisoners were allowed to talk to each other about what course of action they were each going to follow, they would undoubtedly agree to both remain silent. Effective communication and information flow is therefore an essential component of aligning self-interest with decisions that are best for all.

Implied in this scenario, however, is a shared interest in the outcome. Both prisoners want the shortest sentence possible. Add communication into the mix and the right answer for both is almost inevitable.

If the prisoners' interests were not the same, however, then no amount of communication would help. Information flow and a shared purpose are therefore the two key ingredients to effective decision-making.

It takes a little while for employees to fully understand the various issues and change in approach required of them when receiving control. At the same time, it often takes time for owners to come to terms with the changes and to properly let go.

One might imagine this as two glasses, one full of water, one empty. Like the owner slowly feeling able to let go as the team slowly gains confidence, so the water is emptied from one glass to fill the other.

This process takes time. It is for this reason that:

(a) Once decided, the change to the ownership of the company should be discussed and communicated as early as possible.

BUT

(b) The actual change to the ownership should be actioned last; only when the business is already running as if the owner wasn't there will the owner be able to step away.

In this way employees will come to see the advantages of employee ownership, which will impact on the other areas of creating an eternal business; but the change in ownership does not actually happen until the sides to the pyramid are fully built.

This is *not* to say that once the company is in a suitable shape to be made employee-owned that it will be complete. Businesses are never 'finished' – that's part of the fun! Employees of businesses that are employee-owned are always learning and adapting. It is the case, however, that employees need to demonstrate that they are able to successfully run the business in order for an owner to feel able to relinquish control.

One might say that the change to employee ownership is the blueprint drawn up at the very beginning, but is also the last block to go on top of the pyramid, bringing everything together. Start it first, complete it last.

Boiling point

The management consultancy Baxendale started out life in 1866 as a foundry, making railway carriages and gas lamp posts. Through the 20th century this slowly changed to internal boilers. By the 1980s the Baxi Boiler meant that the company was one of the most successful boiler makers in the world.

Philip Baxendale sold the company into an employee trust in 1983. Around 2000, however, Philip had retired and a disastrous acquisition decision by the board meant that the manufacturing business had to be sold.

Philip realised that employee ownership alone would not protect a business from poor decisions. Other aspects of the business also needed to be developed. This knowledge has led to Baxendale morphing into a company that advises businesses on all aspects of how to become employee-owned.

The legal structure represents only one side of the eternal pyramid. It is essential that all four sides are worked on concurrently if the business is to have a chance of thriving in employee ownership – of being eternal.

CONCLUSION

Our eternal pyramid will be built one block at a time from the ground up, each block enabling another block to be added. Focusing on one of the four sides of the pyramid too heavily while ignoring the others creates the danger of an imbalance.

Building equally across the business in this way allows the control to be gently transitioned away from the current owner as it becomes accepted and understood by the employees.

In the ensuing chapters we will look at each side of the pyramid in more detail – but we must always bear in mind the importance of the other sides of the pyramid. How might your activity on one side affect, or be affected by, the other sides?

We do, however, need to start somewhere. First, then, let us make sure we have our flag firmly secured in the ground.

Chapter 3

THE FLAG

INTRODUCTION

The flag side of the eternal pyramid refers to a flag in the ground around which everyone will gather. It is the flag at the front of the parade which everyone follows. It is not only the sense of purpose of the business, it is an alignment of that sense of purpose with the employees who work there; with the clients; with introducers; with anyone who touches the business.

It is the reason why people work for this business when they could choose any other. This clarity of purpose will ensure that the company is still acting in the same way in 50 years' time as it is today.

Having clear vision and values is not enough. The flag refers to how the company *operates*; how this sense of purpose permeates throughout the business in everything it does. In the marketing, the culture, how people deal with each other, in what the business actually produces.

We will look at the concept of the flag by separating the process of creating it into four steps.

THE FLAG

In part 1 we will seek real clarity over what the flag looks like (the vision).

In part 2 we will then look at how to engage all employees with the flag (the principles).

Part 3 will look at how to embed the flag into the business by establishing good processes at important points, such as recruitment.

Finally, in part 4 we will look at ways to ensure the flag is communicated in a consistent manner, both within the business, and to the outside world.

- ○ **Key statement**
- ○ **Key principles**
- ○ **Output**
- ○ **Communications plan**

By the end of this chapter, you will have:

- a key statement summarising your flag from part 1

- a set of key principles which expand on your flag from part 2

- output which illustrates how those key principles are embedded into the processes of the business from part 3

- a communications plan, inspired by the examples in part 4.

PART 1: CAPTURE THE VISION IN A KEY STATEMENT

In many businesses, especially small and medium-sized businesses (SMEs), the sense of purpose is usually provided by one or a few people. The founder with the clear vision, for instance, or the team that sets out with a unified purpose for what they want to achieve.

In transitioning control from the existing owner to the employees, it is crucial that this vision is captured. This will be a key part of allowing the owner to let go.

Remember, each side of the eternal pyramid leans on the others. A flag in the ground means that decision-making can be tested against a common purpose; that the company will attract staff who really want to work for the company; and that ownership of the company will be about servicing that purpose to create long-term sustainable profit.

The flag is important to any business but is *essential* to an eternal business. An eternal business cannot be reliant upon just one person or a small group of people for the simple reason that visionaries will not be around forever. The flag needs to be identified and made real.

The key statement (expressing the flag in simple terms)

There are many ways of expressing the company's vision. It could be a sentence, a white paper, a speech, a book, a video. It does, however, need to be clear and direct, and this means that it needs to be summarised, and that's what this part of the chapter is focused on: producing a headline sentence or two that encapsulates what the business is all about.

We need to be wary of dreaded mission statement waffle. A mission statement is surely the only place where the words 'synergy' and 'paradigm' might appear in the same sentence. Poor mission statements try too hard to impress. They often end up making promises that can't be delivered, or try so hard not to offend that they end up not really saying anything at all.

What you are aiming for is to set down the purpose of the business. It's the answer to the question "What gets you out of bed in the morning?" What makes you choose to work here and not anywhere else (ignoring apathy for a moment!)? It needs to be capable of being summarised in a few lines.

Here's a practical exercise to get you started:

Write down what gets you fired up. If your company were to become eternal, what difference would it make to the world? How would you describe the difference the business makes to its customers? Not what your *type* of business does – what *your* business does.

A few suggestions about your headline:

- Be as specific as possible.

- Don't focus on what you do, but why you do it. (See the works of Simon Sinek.)

- Don't try and perfect it first time – get something down, then come back to it as you work through the rest of this chapter.

- Feel free to make it a few sentences. You can refine the wording later. To begin with you just want to get what's in your heart onto the page.

- Don't try to appeal to everyone. You are creating a flag around which likeminded people will gather. This also means some people will *not* be attracted to it.

Finding your flag

Where she comes across a company that is struggling to identify their flag, Anna Masheter of AM Learning Ltd facilitates a group session that focuses on key questions relating to three stages of the business. Examples of these questions include:

In the beginning:

- How did the business start?
- What was the initial purpose?
- Why was this important?

Today:

- What makes you feel proud?
- What do people say about the business?
- What impact does the business have on its customers?

Future:

- What do you want your customers to say about you that they might not say today?
- What would this mean to you?

What if I don't have a vision?

You do. You just don't know it.

Get some help, engage a business coach, talk to people. Nick someone else's. Read a book. Get it teased out of you. Just make sure the business has a clear vision for others to measure their actions against. Don't over-complicate your vision.

How will you know if your vision is clear enough?

I have been a member of many a committee over the years (with varying degrees of success!). I have been a school governor, a trustee of charities, a non-executive director of companies.

Sometimes I arrive at a meeting not having received, or having had time to read, an agenda or meeting notes. Sometimes I am required to comment on or contribute towards a decision about which I have very little information.

There is one surefire way of getting quickly up to speed in situations like this, and that is to ask the question "How will this decision help achieve the organisation's main objective?"

The clearer the objective of the organisation, the easier it will be to reach good quality decisions in a short space of time. If questions like this are difficult to answer, you need a clearer vision.

As good as Golder

Golder is an employee-owned global consulting company with around 6,500 employees. Its vision was established early on by the three founders in the 1960s. A few years ago the company was facing challenges in the business driven by a downturn in the natural resources market. The CEO brought together a working group of some 200 employee owners to reaffirm the company's long-term destination. The group produced a business plan entitled 'Our Destination', to provide a path forward for the business. This document was then put out to the company as a whole to vote upon with the intent to inspire its people during this difficult time. The plan received overwhelming support.

Two years later and the company was through its difficult patch and returned to strong performance. Having a clear flag not only enabled the working party to map their proposal to a clear objective but also gave the company as a whole a common language with which to discuss its future.

Who should find the vision?

There are many possible sources of the vision. Who to approach will differ depending upon the nature of each business.

The visionary business

Sometimes one or two people have a clear vision which they are able to articulate and which is so strong that it becomes the defining feature of the business.

It may be that the visionary is able to share their vision clearly and simply, that identifying this aspect of the flag is simply a case of asking them. Alternatively the visionary may need the help of another party, such as a coach, to express it with complete clarity and simplicity.

The gap-in-the-market business

Often businesses are established simply because someone sees an opportunity, exploiting a gap in the marketplace. A business set up in reaction to demand in the market will need more time to find and define its vision. The process is more likely to involve a group of people defining the principles.

The business of convenience

A similar problem faces businesses set up to provide support for a group of likeminded individuals. For example, a financial planning practice which is made up of self-employed advisers, each dealing with (and protective of) its own client bank, with a centralised administration function, is not really a business at all.

Such businesses are fine as a temporary home, but in order to be eternal there needs to be a unifying sense of purpose. If a clear vision does arise, a meaningful business can start to emerge and attract likeminded employees.

Going external

So depending on the type of business, the process of finding the vision may come from one, a few or many people within the business. There is, however, one other category of person that might have something to say on the subject of what being a client of your business really means: your clients!

Why not ask your clients what they believe your company represents? If the business has introducers that recommend your company – ask them why. This might not come naturally, but if people enjoy being your customers, they will probably be happy to talk to you about the reasons why.

Conclusion to part 1

Having a clear flag in the ground around which everyone can gather is an essential part of handing over control and becoming an eternal business. How else will employees who are now involved in making real business decisions know that they are making *good* decisions without the flag to map against?

- ☑ **Key statement**
- ◯ **Key principles**
- ◯ **Output**
- ◯ **Communications plan**

The next stage is to make sure that everyone understands what the flag means, and that everything the company does is consistent with those principles.

PART 2: THE SET OF PRINCIPLES THAT ACHIEVE THAT VISION

You have summarised the flag with a few lines pronouncing a vision. But you need to expand this vision in order to outline an attitude – a set of principles.

Ove Arup's key speech

A wonderful example of a clear flag in the ground was provided by Ove Arup, the founder of the design and engineering giant known today as Arup Group Limited. In 1970 he gave a speech to a gathering of the partners of the various parts of the company from around the world. At the time the business was facing a challenge as some of the founding partners were retiring and handing control over to the next generation. In what has become known as 'The Key Speech', Arup outlined:

1.　the aims of the firm

2.　the principles by which those aims might be achieved.

The document is easy to find online (a pdf is available on the Arup website) and remains a remarkable read. It is still given to every new member of staff and debated within Arup on a regular basis.

A good example of a principle (as opposed to a theoretical and unachievable trait) is aim number six, which is the 'Reasonable prosperity of members'. This says, quite clearly, that if you want the possibility of rising to the top of an organisation and earning much more than your peers, don't join Arup. If, however, you want to work in a company that is proud of what it does, and which will share the rewards of its success and your contribution to it, then Arup is for you.

Now that's a *real* flag in the ground!

Involving the employees

An eternal business will be a consistent one. It will be able to demonstrate that the values that lie behind the vision also lie behind the product or service that the company provides. It will also have a flag that is understood and upheld by *everyone* within the business.

It is for this reason that employees should now be invited to contribute if they have not before. Just don't forget the old saying – 'A camel is a horse designed by a committee'. It might only be senior employees who are involved in this stage, or perhaps a few volunteers.

Employees join because they believe in the flag, but they will stay – and accept control – because they have a say in how the flag translates into what they actually do in the company.

Employee engagement is reported by many employee-owned firms to be their biggest challenge. Having a clearly defined flag to gather around, and then allowing employees a genuine part in turning that flag into the client experience, can make a huge difference to how engaged employees are within a business.

The principles of John Lewis's flag

The John Lewis Partnership is the UK's largest example of an employee-owned business where all 84,000 staff are Partners in the business. Comprising 50 John Lewis and 353 Waitrose shops, their employees are called 'Partners', and the company is structured around seven Principles.

Key to these Principles is Principle 1: "The Partnership's ultimate purpose is the happiness of all its members, through their worthwhile and satisfying employment in a successful business."

David Jones is a Waitrose board member and Partnership Registrar and is responsible for ensuring the business upholds these Principles through three key activities: assure, influence and support. This means he deals with Partners on a daily basis, and through the Partnership's Democratic channels helps communicate the board strategy throughout the company.

One key approach that David adopts in these discussions is that he is not passing around information – he is sharing knowledge. He doesn't just want the Partners to know what the board has been discussing and deciding, he wants them to know why.

The key principles

Coming up with a pithy one liner was probably not easy, and in doing so much can be lost. In order to develop the key statement into a set of principles, we could start with asking ourselves the following question: *what characteristics typify that vision?*

You are seeking to identify a set of key principles that will tell people what the company is all about. Like the key statement, these are unlikely to change significantly over time. These are the principles which expound the vision. Future business decisions will be mapped against these principles.

You are not looking for 'We want to be the best' type statements. You are seeking a filter. It should deter some people from joining as much as it attracts others.

Comparing actual with the theoretical – an exercise

You have asked your employees and your customers what gets them animated. You've challenged yourself to find examples that prove that the business acts in accordance with those principles. To reiterate, the result we are looking for is a line or two summarising the purpose, followed by a list of principles which prove how the business delivers that purpose.

Here is another practical exercise to help identify the key principles which typify the flag. (It might be a good exercise when involving senior employees or volunteers.) Buy a few packets of blank postcards. Post-it notes will also work. Write down every type of impact of the business, one per postcard. **What happens as a result of your company existing?** Internal and external impacts, on both employees and clients. Come up with as many outputs as you can.

Now take this big pile of postcards and spread them out on a large table or the floor. Are there any obvious themes? Can they be grouped into piles, into a small number of categories? Are there common themes?

You will now have a smaller number of piles of cards. Place another blank postcard on top of each pile and write a few words summarising what each pile represents. You might be able to group one or two more piles together at this point.

You now have a set of key principles. Take these top cards and spread them out. Are there any principles that are *not* covered? Keep refining and working on these principles, until you can narrow it down to a shortlist (no specific number, but anything above, say, eight would fail to provide the required clarity).

The key principles: prove it

One test of whether the vision and principles are clear enough is to imagine a new employee on their first day – in 50 years' time. Hopefully they chose to work for this company. There were other jobs that paid more, but this is the job they really wanted. They know that working for this company will allow them to achieve things that really matter to them.

How have they reached this conclusion? What have they seen or read about that made them apply for the job in the first place? When they arrive on their first day, what will they see or hear that will confirm to them that they have made the right choice?

Here's a simple exercise to find out just how far a business puts the claims made by the flag into practice. This could be a group exercise with a flip chart or a whiteboard.

Step 1: List your principles. (Or gather the cards or pieces of paper with them on, if you followed the previous exercise.)

Step 2: Now prove it. Where is the evidence that proves the company acts in accordance with its stated vision and principles? This doesn't mean a survey – it means writing down as many things as possible that the company does which are a direct consequence of the flag.

Holding a 'prove it' session will bring about a process of introspection which can lead to a greater understanding of what is actually good about the business. It can help to clarify the principles but, perhaps more importantly, it will lead to further ways in which the flag will be embedded into the business.

"So prove it."

Many years ago I was sat with Geoff Cole, managing partner of a large local firm of accountants. I was explaining to Geoff all the reasons why he should recommend Ovation to his clients. He sat patiently, listening to the list of ways in which I thought my offering was different to those of my competitors.

When I had finished, Geoff said to me "Chris, I have no doubt that you are different from the others, that all you have told me is true. However, everyone else tells me the same thing. So prove it."

Prove it. Those two words have stayed with me ever since. I went away and spent time thinking about how I could prove everything I said. I came up with a list of statistics and facts, such as how much of our income comes from existing clients, that we hadn't lost a client for five years, and so on.

Having to prove it helped me to understand what I was really doing – it helped me gain clarity around my flag.

The process also made me realise that when I made a statement about an outcome, there was invariably a process that produced that outcome. It helped me to define the service proposition of my business.

I presented my 'prove it' presentation to Geoff. He began to introduce clients, became a client himself, as well as a close friend.

Conclusion to part 2

You should now have: a key statement that summarises why the business exists; a series of key principles elaborating on that statement. The key statement is unlikely to change. The key principles are also unlikely to change, however they should be reviewed when necessary, for example due to changing market conditions.

☑ **Key statement**
☑ **Key principles**
◯ **Output**
◯ **Communications plan**

How much is this vision understood and shared by everyone in the business? By clients? For a business to be eternal, the flag needs to run through the business like the proverbial stick of Blackpool rock. The principles held so dear by the owner and employees need to be reflected in what the business produces, and how it is produced.

In other words, the flag has to be planted in the soil of the business. There are processes which do this. Undertaking these processes with all employees should improve engagement and tip the transition of control further in their direction.

PART 3: PROCESSES WHICH IMPLEMENT THE FLAG

An eternal business will be a consistent one. It will be able to demonstrate that the values that lie behind the vision also lie behind everything that happens within the business.

An eternal business will put into practice the principles espoused by the flag. It will live and breathe those principles in all that it says and does – and not just in front of the client!

The flag is like a beacon, sending out messages to the world for everyone to gather round. What they find when they arrive must be the same as what attracted them in the first place.

You now should have a headline key statement, and a series of key principles. The final stage is to outline the characteristics of the company that will uphold those principles. First we'll take a look at how the flag runs through the processes and procedures within the business; then we'll take some time to consider how the flag affects the employees of the business.

The flag running through the business

A business with a clear sense of purpose will have something which people will want to be part of. Employees will want to work there, customers will want to buy from it. This will be a business that a founder will feel able to leave in the hands of the employees.

It is therefore essential that the company acts according to its vision. Not only does the product or service it delivers need to be consistent with the values of the business, but also how it is promoted. For example, perhaps the employees could debate the following questions:

- How does the company deliver its service in the way that the marketing promises?

- How does the company treat the employees in the same way it treats its customers and clients?

Let's look at a few activities to involve all employees while at the same time testing the consistency of the flag throughout the business.

Look around you!

A good test of a vision is to ask someone to talk about it. How often have you been at a business networking event and had someone explain to you what their business does, how they are 'different from the rest', when the business was founded. Then perhaps the conversation ran dry and you asked them about their weekend. Suddenly they become animated! Their eyes light up and they begin to use their arms as they talk about something that they are passionate about.

What is it about the business that gets you – the owner and employees – animated when you tell others about it? It certainly won't be how many years the company has been in existence for!

Ask people to explain what the business does, what they do within the business. Observe what gets them animated – the answers might come as a pleasant surprise to a founder. Ask clients the same questions. What has got them excited and grateful? Make a note of these moments. Do they have anything in common? Are they aligned in some way to the flag?

The output from this exercise could be a few paragraphs explaining what it is the company actually does, in each area of operation. It could be video testimonials for the website. It is important, however, that all such output can clearly be linked back to the flag and the key principles.

Treating staff and clients the same

The extent to which a vision is realised throughout a business can be demonstrated by how it treats its employees. If a company says part of its core mission is to be 'the best company to work for' and is then found to pay lower than the minimum wage, the flag is shown to be a sham and will ultimately not be successful in attracting the desired staff and customers.

Such a business can, of course, be successful. However it is far more likely to be one that focuses on increasing shareholder value than long-term sustainable profit. As such, it is less likely to be an eternal business.

Most companies will survey their clients and (hopefully) take action from the results. Why not do the same with employees? The eternal business will be an employee-owned business, and as such should be an extremely open environment, where employee opinion is actively sought.

Measuring the wellbeing of employees

Wellbeing in the workplace has become a major focus for many companies and seems unlikely to go away. Companies have realised that to repeat the mantra that 'Our company is our staff' is not enough – they need to act upon it.

Happy City UK (**www.happycity.org.uk**) provides a wellbeing tool for measuring the wellbeing of employees. This firstly enables companies to assess current levels of wellbeing; then to develop a targeted wellbeing policy; then to measure again in, say, a year's time to assess the success of their actions.

In this way employers can demonstrate that they really do care about their employees as much as they care about their customers.

Business processes: prove it

We want to make sure the business processes follow the key principles and are aligned with the key statement. For example, if one of the principles was innovation, where is this demonstrated within the operations of the business?

To achieve this we can perform the same exercise as we did with regards to the service proposition, namely:

Step 1: Write out the main procedures within the business (down to granular level if you have the time, but more likely to be the main activities).

Step 2: Now prove it. Where is the evidence that proves these processes contribute towards the flag?

Again, the precise nature of this output is for the business (preferably the employees) to decide. It should, however, clearly demonstrate how the business operates in accordance with each of the key principles – at least one item of output for each principle. These outputs should be reviewed and tested on a regular basis.

Note – process mapping is a skill in itself, and not one that everyone possesses. External help may go a long way with many parts of building an eternal business, and no more than at this stage in the process.

Eternal employees

An eternal business requires product or service delivery towards a shared vision. It needs consistency of delivery, a common sense of purpose. It requires the employees and advisers to the business to share the core values that are summarised by the flag. Most importantly, those employees and advisers will understand the importance of sharing those core values.

This is nicely summarised in a paragraph from the book *On Form* by ex-England cricket captain and psychoanalyst Mike Brearley. Considering what circumstances tend to lead to a team being 'on form', he says:

> "When on form, [teams] are creative, effective, coordinated. They are not dominated by selfish individualism, nor has individual flair been suppressed. The team's morale is properly positive, neither complacent nor rent with excessive rivalry and doubt. Though its members are not always in emotional harmony with each other, they share a common purpose and are able to set aside differences…"

Recruitment

Recruitment is going to be key in order to attract employees who share the same core values. A strong vision well-disseminated should attract the right type of people. But a successful business which shares those successes with its employees is likely to attract other types as well.

The key is to build the flag into the recruitment process. Many years ago I summarised the characteristics that typified the 'Ovation Way' in a 'What Defines Ovation' document. This described the sort of qualities that an Ovation employee would be expected to show: how the flag translates into employee characteristics. For example, that we believe that there is more to life than money, and that success is not measured in purely financial terms. This is true of how we run our business, as well as what we do for clients.

The broken umbrella

Our office for many years was reached by walking up a few steps from the road, along a short path, then up some more steps to the front door. As I left the office one evening I noticed a broken umbrella on the path. Any client coming into the office would have to step over that umbrella.

A few things had been happening that had left me a bit grumpy, so, as a test, I left the umbrella. I came in late the next morning. The umbrella was still there. After putting it in the bin, I called a staff meeting. I asked who had seen the umbrella. Everyone mumbled or nodded that they had. I then asked why no one had picked it up. No one replied.

By stepping over it, they each accepted that it was OK for the first thing the client sees as they ascend the steps towards our office to be a broken umbrella. By doing nothing, they had given their approval. This was not the Ovation way.

The objective of the recruitment process is for both employer and prospective employee to identify whether an individual is a good match both for the company and for the role. It is not a test of character. It is for this reason that lying on a CV or in an interview is completely nonsensical and self-defeating.

The recruitment process for an eternal business should involve as many of the employees as possible/appropriate. If anyone should be able to spot 'one of them' it should be the existing team.

Diversity

Having said that the flag should attract potential employees who have the core values that the business wants, it is also important that the recruitment policy encourages diversity.

We all have a tendency to recruit people that we like, or perhaps that are like us (often the same thing!). Known as the 'halo effect', we warm to the familiar, to the comfortable. As a consequence, there is a danger that mapping recruiting decisions against the flag might prevent the company employing people who could offer different perspectives and points of view.

Awareness of the issue; involving many employees in the interview process; having more than one interview; and perhaps using outside help are all ways of encouraging diversity in the workplace.

The 'my client' mentality

One of the biggest drags on a service business that is trying to create and disseminate a unified sense of purpose is the 'my client' mentality. Businesses made up of individuals working solely on their own client banks and earning according to their own efforts are sometimes called 'Eat what you kill' businesses. Actually, they aren't really businesses at all, let alone entities that have the potential to last forever; they are a collection of individuals doing their own thing. Often the people involved are building up their own client bank ready to leave and set up their own businesses.

Clients of an eternal business are clients of a working business, not of an individual. This might not sit well with certain people. That's fine. The sort of person that thinks they 'own' a client is not going to be someone who will fit in with an eternal business.

The isolated clients

I once attended a compliance supervisor's course. We were discussing individual competencies, and one compliance officer proudly told us of his spreadsheet that he had created to monitor the training and competence of the 45 self-employed advisers he was responsible for. It listed all the advisers along the top and all the areas of learning along the side. When someone passed an exam, he ticked the relevant box.

I asked if advisers shared clients, and he replied that no, everyone owned their own client banks. I then asked if anyone had every box ticked, and he confirmed none had. I then suggested that not one of his advisers should be allowed to see a client. Slightly annoyed, he asked me to explain myself.

I said that if none of the self-employed advisers allowed their clients to speak to other advisers, and yet were not trained in all areas, how could those clients be adequately advised? If an adviser had not passed competency in pensions, for example, that meant their clients would not receive advice on pensions. How could that be right?

The organiser of the course politely – and quickly – thanked me for my contribution and moved on to the next slide.

Extrapolating this suggests that those who are more driven by financial rewards and personal success, by competition and doing things 'their way', will tend to be attracted to 'Eat what you kill' businesses. This might mean that the more successful sales people – the 'hunters' – will *not* be attracted to an eternal business.

This does not need to be the case. It is still possible to reward sales through traditional methods within an eternal business. It is the profits that will be shared, in a way that will be agreed upon by all employees. If one person thinks they deserve a high bonus before the profit-share calculations, perhaps because of high sales, then they should be prepared to justify this to the rest of the team.

Induction

Once the new employee starts work, induction into an eternal business is also essential. Detail on what makes for an excellent induction process are not for this book, however one that suits an eternal business should certainly include:

- discussion of the flag, what it means to different people, and how it is represented throughout the business

- understanding the decision-making processes, and how the new employee might be expected/able to contribute to decisions

- how life in an employee-owned business differs from other businesses.

Inducting freelancers the right way

The animation studio Aardman frequently uses freelancers, engaging with many of their staff on a temporary contract basis for particular projects (the movie *Early Man*, say, or a *Wallace and Gromit* short).

The company takes these relationships extremely seriously, however, and considers their freelancers to be very much part of the team. As such the recruitment and induction process for a freelancer is designed to ensure that they understand the values and culture of the business.

As a result, many of the freelancers return to work on different projects, providing the consistency of creative output that has given the company its enviable reputation.

Conclusion to part 3

You should now have a key statement; key principles which expand that statement; and output which illustrates how those principles translate into how the company operates.

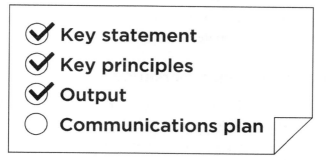

✓ **Key statement**
✓ **Key principles**
✓ **Output**
○ **Communications plan**

The final stage is to make sure that the flag is communicated to clients, existing employees, new employees, existing clients, prospective clients, introducers, consultants and advisers and the world at large in a clear and consistent manner.

PART 4: A COMMUNICATION STRATEGY THAT CLEARLY EXPOUNDS THE FLAG (AKA MARKETING AND BRANDING)

You have the flag – you now need to stick it in the ground so that people who see themselves as being aligned to your vision and values will gather round it.

There are gazillions of books about marketing and building a brand that you should read. This section is *not* intended to tell you how to turn your clear business vision and values into a marketing strategy. Suffice it to say that the clearer you can communicate that vision, the more clients will want to be part of your 'gang'.

There are, however, methods of communication that might be of particular benefit to an eternal business. In this section we'll look at what other companies have done and share some ideas for you to pick and choose from – and be inspired by – when compiling your own communications strategy.

Centrally controlled marketing

As much as possible the marketing of the company should be controlled centrally. This allows for a unified vision and will ensure that the message being sent out is consistent.

Of course, 'centrally' doesn't necessarily mean a group at head office who have no experience of life at the coal face. Our definition of 'centrally' means one marketing plan for the business, which might have been developed by interested parties from various parts of the business. All 'centrally' means in this context is that the approach is agreed and applied in a consistent way across the business.

A good sales team should thrive in such an environment. The central marketing should provide the tools for the sales team.

Here are a few examples of marketing that can and should be controlled centrally:

- branding and brand/reputation (how the flag is translated into key messages and values for marketing)
- website
- literature
- social media (to a point)
- events
- outgoing communications
- director profiles
- surveys
- testimonials
- processes for the service proposition
- sponsorship
- charities.

There are some areas of marketing that cannot be controlled centrally, and these might include:

- independent socialising
- what employees actually say (although if the other sides of the eternal pyramid are in place, keeping employees 'on message' should not present a problem)
- some social media.

Touchpoints

One way of ensuring that the message the business communicates is consistent is by having a variety of different touchpoints with clients.

Clients and prospective clients should have regular contact with the company. Clearly these should not be intrusive or annoying, but at a level appropriate to the nature of the product or service. Ideally these touchpoints should be on a *regular basis* from *different people* within the firm. This is particularly important if the nature of your service is such that the client receives regular advice from one individual – it will help avoid the 'my client' situation developing.

These touchpoints should also be different in nature, reflecting the stage the client may have reached in considering becoming a client (see *Watertight Marketing* by Bryony Thomas). For example, a client's very first exposure to the business will be short and elicit an emotional reaction. They will then start to require more information and make a more measured assessment.

As the prospective client is brought into the business, the face-to-face activity is likely to be predominantly with one main point of contact (account manager, partner, adviser, consultant, etc). It is important, however, that the prospect feels they are becoming a client of the business as a whole. There are plenty of opportunities to create touchpoints with other members of the team:

- receiving the initial enquiry
- setting up the initial meetings
- pre-marketing/contracting (for example, an email saying, "We're looking forward to meeting you, here's a bit about the team.")
- meet at your office
- have them met at reception by another member of the team

- after the meeting issue a "Nice to meet you, here's how we can help you" letter from the main point of contact, but sent by another member of the team.

Once the client has been brought fully on board there are many ways of keeping in touch. This provides further opportunities to make them feel part of the company, and not just the client of the one person they might deal with regularly. Examples of these touchpoints for existing clients might include:

- providing a newsletter on, say, a quarterly basis, sent from a named person

- newsletter content to include updates on what is happening in the business, e.g. new qualifications, births, company in the community, recruitment, social events (quiz nights, trips to the theatre, expert briefings)

- hosting networking events (help business clients to strengthen their own businesses)

- surveys

- updates on activity from someone other than the main point of contact

- activities in the community, e.g. sponsor the local junior cricket team.

Bespoke service

An employee leaving your eternal business should find it nigh on impossible to replicate your service in order to attract clients away. That means providing a level and style of service which would mean the client would perceive themselves to be clearly disadvantaged should they move away. Examples of these might include:

- client portal (for example, allowing a client to access the information that you hold about them)

- document storage (for example, a legal practice which keeps hold of the client's wills)

- a spread of skills and knowledge across the firm

- different people having different areas of expertise, so that clients don't get all their information from one person

- introductory services (for example links to associated services).

The unexpected benefits of our financial planning

As a financial planning firm, Ovation helps clients to work out what they want from life, then creates a forecast to assess whether they are financially on track to reach that future.

Often the conclusion to this planning is that clients actually have more money than they need for the happy life they envisioned. The conclusion is either to give some money away, or to spend it.

As a consequence we are often in the position that, as well as managing their money, we also help them to spend it. When we discuss what people would like to do more of, the most popular response is travel.

We therefore have an arrangement with a bespoke travel agency called C The World. They have helped clients to go kayaking in the Norwegian fjords, samurai sword fighting in Osaka, Japan, and helped a wheelchair-bound client to go to places he and his wife didn't think was possible.

This is not what people tend to expect from a financial planning company, and yet it is an outcome that is very much appreciated.

"We're not like the rest"

How often have you heard that expression from someone whose firm is actually *just* like all the rest? If the business is really not like the rest, it will be acting in a way that truly represents a unique vision. This is *really* doing things differently!

Here are just a few examples of how some companies make themselves stand out from their competitors:

- published service standards that are consistent throughout the company AND examples of improvements where the standards have not been met

- the solicitor who is a keen runner and invites clients to go running with him

- the business adviser who conducts meetings while walking around London

- telephoning not emailing

- the ecommerce software company that invites customers and their families to camp with them at the WOMAD festival

- the accountant who selects a 'client of the month' and sends them homemade cakes

- the consultant who sends letters rather than emails

- the company that has client testimonials as a live feed on the website, so that ALL responses are shown

- the company that sends a copy of the book *Jonathan Livingston Seagull* to every new client

- the financial planner who sends a postcard to clients showing an aged version of their face, with the message "Looking forward to helping you plan towards when you look like this!"

Clients meeting clients

There is a particular advantage in getting clients to meet with other clients. One objective of an eternal business is to create a community with a shared sense of purpose. Hopefully a client's buying decision was made because there was a matching of core values between the client and the business.

It should therefore be logical that if clients have similar values to your business, they are also likely to share those core values with each other. Once clients meet each other, therefore, this should bring about a feeling of camaraderie, and help create a community around the business.

Bringing clients together

Many firms hold regular events for clients and other contacts of the company to meet each other, and to meet all the employees. This could take the form of theatre trips, Christmas drinks or putting on a speaker.

One firm has one particular rule at their events. They insist that attendees do not talk business, either with them or with each other.

The managing director overheard an accountant and a solicitor talking about a mutual client. He interrupted the conversation, and, laughing, reminded the two attendees – both good introducers of work to the business – of the golden rule: no talking shop.

Five minutes later he walked past again, only to hear the business conversation had resumed. The managing director took out a yellow card that he had brought to the event for this purpose, brandished it towards the accountant and solicitor, and marched one to the other side of the room where he introduced them to a client.

As the managing director comments, "When you don't allow people to talk about business, it is amazing just how much business results!"

The magic of the meeting room

Your meeting room can reflect significantly on the values of your business. For example, a large table with upright chairs and nothing on the walls could be considered professional, but it could also feel cold. Is this impression consistent with the flag?

The merits of a stately home boardroom

I used to work for a company that had offices at a prestigious location in central London. As clients came into the office they were greeted by the site of an antique staircase stretching off to the right, then walked a few paces along the plush carpet to be greeted by the receptionist sat behind an old wooden desk covered with green leather.

Meetings took place in the boardroom. This was a large oak-panelled room with oil paintings around the walls. The boardroom table was a 22-leaf antique oak dining table, and we sat on chairs that wouldn't have been out of place in a stately home.

Almost every client who was visiting us for the first time expressed a reaction to their surroundings. Half puffed their chest out a little, as if to say, 'Oh yes, these are my advisers. This is the sort of place that I should be seen in.'

The other half had a different reaction, best summarised by a client called Brian, who took one look round the boardroom and said: "Huh. So this is where my fees go."

The meeting room is often the place where clients have the largest insight into the culture of a company. It is a huge opportunity to connect with clients and secure the meeting of core values – or to filter out those clients who *don't* share your core values.

For example, what values does the following meeting room suggest: clients have the option of sitting on sofas or at a modern table; a guitar sits in the corner; on the walls are two paintings of the local area by a client, one of them of the outside of that very office. Fresh coffee and tea is brewing, in the corner is a fridge containing water and other cold drinks. A bookshelf holds books personally picked by each employee.

All of these touches are entirely deliberate. They convey the culture of the company.

Creating culture in the canteen

Although not an employee-owned business, Yeo Valley dairy has gone to extraordinary lengths to create the culture it wants within its business. It has achieved this by way of the staff canteen.

Situated in the Mendip Hills in Somerset, the head office has stunning views. The staff canteen serves restaurant-quality food in a room that can, as a minimum, be described as funky! A mural of The Beatles adorns one meeting room wall, bright colours are everywhere, umbrellas act as light shades.

The canteen has been opened to the public, who eat with the employees during lunch. It also opens in the evenings and gets booked up many months in advance.

The employees take great pride in their canteen, which is seen as the heart of what it is like to work

> for Yeo Valley. It was even featured on a television programme in 2017. As boss Tim Mead said, "There's an old farming expression, if you look after the land, the land looks after you. If you look after the cows, the cows look after you. And if you look after your staff, your staff will look after you."

Thanks to great strides in technology, it is no longer necessary to see clients in the office at all. Video conferencing means the many hours spent travelling to see clients (or for them to see you) is no longer necessary.

However, holding a client meeting by telephone or video means that all these touches in the meeting room are lost. In addition, the clients don't get to meet other members of the team, and the subtleties of body language are lost.

Of course, video conferencing is more convenient, and may well be preferred by some clients. But at what cost?

Messaging

The essence of a communications strategy for an eternal business is that it must get across the flag in such a way that it will attract clients (as well as future employees) with the same core values. What messages are being sent to ensure that this is the case?

An interesting exercise to answer this question can be to map out the route from what clients *want* to what clients *value*.

These are not always the same thing. It is an old marketing cliché that clients don't buy a drill, they buy a hole. Well I'd actually take that further. I'm terrible at DIY, utterly uninterested. In the unlikely event I go shopping for a drill, I'm not even buying a hole, I'm buying somewhere I can screw a bracket into for a shelf. And I'm not actually buying a shelf, I'm buying a place to put my books. I could, of course, gift my books to a charity shop, but I think they look good on the wall. Added to that is the fact that I loathe DIY, so I actually want to use that drill for as short a time as I can get away with! I'm therefore not buying a drill; I want something that will help me look cool, with as minimal fuss as possible. That's what will determine my buying decision.

We went through the following process at Ovation, an exercise that might prove to be useful to try in your business.

Our company slogan is "Helping people use their wealth to accumulate life, not the other way around." This reflects a belief that money is merely an enabler and not an end itself (hence my *Financial Wellbeing* book and podcast).

However, insight into their future and understanding their own attitude towards money is not generally what drives the majority of our customers to come to us in the first place. What they want is generally something much more specific:

WHAT THEY WANT:
A SPECIFIC QUESTION ANSWERED

Retirement Advice	Investments	Planning

Of course, your firm or sector could have more than three.

We asked ourselves: "What is the question that they are seeking to answer?" This is tough, as there are many variations, but we boiled it down to the following:

**WHAT THEY WANT:
A SPECIFIC QUESTION ANSWERED**

Retirement Advice	Investments	Planning
When Can I?	Do It Properly	How Much Is Enough?

Then we tried to boil this down further. In answering that question, what would the client gain? What would be the one thing they would come away feeling they had, which they did not have before they entered our office?

**WHAT THEY WANT:
A SPECIFIC QUESTION ANSWERED**

Retirement Advice	Investments	Planning
When Can I?	Do It Properly	How Much Is Enough?
Knowledge	Reassurance	Clarity

Next we wondered what would the client walk away with as a result of their interaction with our service. What would be the *outcome?*

**WHAT THEY WANT:
A SPECIFIC QUESTION ANSWERED**

Retirement Advice	Investments	Planning
When Can I?	Do It Properly	How Much Is Enough?

Knowledge	Reassurance	Clarity
Decision	Trust	Options

Finally, in, say, five years' time, when the client is regarded as a 'loyal' client, what is it that we do that they keep coming back for? After all, they've had their initial question answered, so why do they remain a client and paying fees?

WHAT THEY WANT:
A SPECIFIC QUESTION ANSWERED

Retirement Advice	Investments	Planning
When Can I?	Do It Properly	How Much Is Enough?
Knowledge	Reassurance	Clarity
Decision	Trust	Options
Identifiable Objectives	Peace of Mind	A Clear Path

WHAT THEY GET:
FINANCIAL WELLBEING

Using their wealth to accumulate life

We now can see the path that clients take from a prospect with a question, to a loyal client who will be with the company forever.

The communications plan

The question which brings these various points together is this: what is the messaging from *your* marketing and branding which a) appeals to the prospect, and b) prepares them for being a loyal client?

The final output for the flag is to produce a communications plan which covers the points raised in this section. Then the only thing left to do is to implement that plan!

CONCLUSION

You should now have all parts of the flag complete:

Now is a good moment to issue a reminder: the four sides of the eternal pyramid need to be worked on together. Establishing the flag must be accompanied by the building of the other three sides of the eternal pyramid.

For example, some or all of the employees will be involved in coming up with this communications plan, therefore developing collective decision-making is key. Let us therefore now look at how to devolve decision-making throughout the business in order to get genuinely collaborative decisions.

Chapter 4

HOW TO MAKE ETERNAL DECISIONS

INTRODUCTION

There are many ways for businesses to make decisions. Top-down, bottom-up, hierarchical, flat. I liked to believe my own style when building Ovation Finance was that of a 'benevolent dictatorship'!

Many owner-managed businesses will have the majority of business-affecting decisions made by one person. Even where there is more than one director it is very often one person who has the final say. This is often because of the forceful character of that person, not because it is necessarily the best way to make decisions.

An eternal business will be employee-owned. There is only one rule about decision-making in such a business – it must, to some degree, be devolved away from one person to a group of people. This is not because 'benevolent dictatorship' is necessarily flawed. Rather, it is because the loss of the one decision-maker could mean the end of the business.

Control must be passed from the existing owner to the new owners: the employees.

Introducing chaos – for a higher cause

In 1966, designer and engineer Max Fordham set up his own practice, working from a spare bedroom in his Camden home. His building services and engineering company now has five offices around the UK, with more than 220 employees.

In a charming video on their website, Professor Fordham talks about their story as an employee-owned business. As he puts it, "It is not a profit-sharing business, it's a responsibility-sharing business".

When they first moved to a form of employee ownership, they took the approach that if someone was accepted by their peers to join the company, they should also be accepted as a partner in the business. Their slogan was: "Fit to be an employee, fit to be a partner."

Perhaps the most revealing moment in the video, however, is when Professor Fordham admits that following his innovative ideas of sharing ownership did lead to some confusion within the business. "I had introduced chaos, and it had to be tidied up," he says.

These days the company has clear decision-making structures which give all employees the opportunity to have a say in the running of the business.

Eternal businesses make decisions in a way that involves many, if not all, employees. (Whether this 'involvement' equates to comments and feedback or allowing direct input on decisions will depend on factors such as the size of the business.)

For many employees this will be the first time they have had a real say in business issues. For many owners it will be the first time they have had to accept decisions they might not agree with.

Both parties may find this process a challenge! Part of the solution comes in implementing systems which give real clarity over how to gather the views of employees and who actually makes the decisions. For example, the role of the leadership team could be to harvest the opinions of employees in order that they can make decisions (we'll look at this in more detail when we look at who controls the company in part 2 of chapter 6).

In this chapter we will look at: the mindset change that is required firstly by owners, then by employees, during the change towards employee ownership; some decision-making structures; and finally how to create an environment in which employees will want to contribute towards business decisions.

APPROACHING COLLABORATIVE DECISION-MAKING

Employee engagement is crucial to a business truly benefiting from employee ownership. Collaborative decision-making will only work if employees really believe their voice is being heard and acted upon.

Remember the principle of the pyramid – each of the four sides leans on the others. The

DECISION-MAKING

extent to which employees are engaged with **decision-making** will affect how inspired they are working for the business (**the flag**); how they share in the success of the business (**ownership**); and the clarity they have over how working for this business helps them to achieve their personal objectives (**engaged employees**).

Unleashing potential through employee initiative

There was a company that manufactured and distributed a number of different electronic devices used in a range of healthcare applications. The company was still wholly owned by its founder. It was profitable but many working there felt that it was underachieving and that it would benefit from fresh energy to realise its potential.

Discussions with the founder revealed that he wished to step back from running the company and was also ready to sell his shares. A deal was agreed for an employee ownership trust to buy his shares.

Only one year later and the ownership change had very quickly unleashed an enormous new energy and commitment from employees. This, combined with a strong leadership team, resulted in a 20% revenue increase and a 15% growth in profits in the first year alone.

Source: With thanks to Robert Postlethwaite of Postlethwaite's Solicitors Ltd

Let us start by looking at how we can create an environment in which employees will *want* to get involved with decision-making.

The mindset

Most business owners were, at one point, employees. Indeed, they were probably the type of employee eager to get involved with the running of the business and hoping to reap the rewards. However, that may well have been many years ago.

Most employees have never run a business.

That's not to say that the employees are the ones who face the biggest challenge when a business transitions control to employees. It is as big a leap to leave your business in the hands of someone else as it is to take on the responsibility of owning a business.

What *is* important is that both parties **realise that such a leap is necessary for both parties** in order that a business might become eternal.

The mindset of both parties to this process is key. They need to come together to realise that there are not winners and losers, but something new to be created for the mutual benefit of everyone. It is also important to understand the difference between ownership and control – I might own a pet cat, but that doesn't mean to say that I get to control what it does!

US politician Al Gore summed the process up rather nicely. He was referring to the challenge of climate change, but he could equally be referring to the process of making a business eternal when he said:

"It's not a problem to be solved, it's a dilemma to be managed."

The first step is to realise that this process needs to be taken slowly, at a pace that brings everyone along together. As has been mentioned before (and will be again), the actual sale of the business needs to be decided early but actioned last. The business only completes the transition to employee ownership when the employees are ready to receive it and the owner is able to let go.

Change just means using different tools

When business coach Catrin MacDonnell works with people who are taking on new responsibilities, she asks them to imagine that they have a toolbox which has all the characteristics needed for them to take on that new role.

The employee considers the tools they currently use – e.g. organisation, time management, persuasion etc. – and asks themselves which further tools will they need to select when they take on the new role. This could include proactive thinking, analysis, coaching etc.

Some of these tools they may be able to just pull out and start using, others may need developing through training.

The process requires the employee to identify what is needed to think like a business owner. They will generally realise that they already have some characteristics that work and others that they just need to practise or be trained in.

Most importantly, however, it demonstrates that change only means that we are using different tools.

Let's take a moment to look at some of the specific challenges that people face during the shift of control that happens when a business owned by one or a few individuals changes to one that is owned by employees.

First, let's look at the change in mindset for the owner, then we'll take a similar approach to employees.

OWNERS: IT'S NOT ALL ABOUT YOU ANY MORE

There are many misconceptions about owning and running a business. For example, that you have more control over your destiny – or that you have more freedom of time. Even that you want to be running a business in the first place!

In truth, many business owners feel trapped. If an employee is unhappy in their job, they can always get a new job. For an owner who has sunk time, money and reputation into building their business, this is usually not an option. Being a boss can be very lonely indeed.

Indeed, there is a big difference between being a business owner and being an entrepreneur. One definition might be that entrepreneurs are people who like to invest in – to buy and sell – businesses. Business owners, however, are people who started doing something they had a passion for and years later found themselves running a business!

A chance to go back to what you enjoyed

Tony Yarrow sold a majority stake of his business, Wise Investments, to a trust fund for the benefit of his employees in 2014.

For him, one of the advantages was changing his own role in the business. As he says: "I started off doing something I enjoyed. Then, as the business grew, I ended up running the business. The truth is, no one really wants to run a business, unless that's something they are specifically trained to do. When I sold the business to the employees I changed my role so that I was once again doing what I had done in the first place."

For the founder of a business, therefore, making the business eternal provides the chance to go back to doing the things that you enjoy.

A lot of people *think* that they want to move into management or to run a business until the time comes when they have actually made that move. Then it dawns on them that it isn't what they expected. They begin to long for the days when they used to do the thing that they first started (or joined) the company to do.

Trouble is, this would mean handing over something they have worked so hard to build.

This is one of many reasons why letting go of control is such a challenge. On the one hand, it can be a blessed relief. On the other, the owner needs to feel those eager to take control are able to do so.

The business owner truly letting go of control can therefore be one of the biggest problems for many succession plans.

A message to 'the boss'

Your business has kept on track because of your vision and belligerence. Others may have questioned you over the years, both within and outside the business. You will have had moments where you stood your ground on key decisions, sometimes being the only person who could see the obvious. And when it turns out you are right all along, no one says 'well done'. No one congratulates you on your foresight. It can be a thankless task, being visionary.

Yours has been a benevolent dictatorship. One of the primary reasons your business has succeeded is because it followed the path you set for it.

But, remember, in order for your business to become eternal, ***you need to become the least important person in your business.***

This may seem counter-intuitive. In my experience, most business owners tend to make themselves the *most* important person in their business. They often like it that way, at the same time as bemoaning the fact that they can't get staff they can trust. But as the accountancy firm Burton Sweet says in one of its brochures:

Are you proud of working weekends?

Why?

If you, the business owner, are the most important person in your business, how can you sell the business? No one will want to buy your business if the most important asset is going to be lost.

In order to remove yourself from the business, something needs to replace that benevolent dictator.

Replacing yourself

Note I said some*thing*, not some*one*. Many business owners have gone down the route of replacing themselves with another managing director. This simply changes the reliance of the business from one individual to another.

Changing the culture and infrastructure of a business takes time and effort, but there are clear paths and people who can help. A business owner stepping aside, however, is something that only that owner can do – so it needs to start with the will to do so.

Most of this book is about how to get the business in shape so that it is able to survive without you. But of equal importance is getting *you* in shape so that you can survive without the business! Like Mike and Charlotte Procter in chapter 1, this means working out what life might look like – and building a financial plan to get there – to ensure that you will be pulled into life after the business, and not pushed.

The founder's motivation

Peter Worthing established Worthing and Leeds 25 years ago, with Bob Leeds. Bob sold out to Peter after 15 years. Aged 67, Peter retained a controlling interest and was company chairman. The business had 85 staff, six of which were on the board.

These directors were becoming increasingly frustrated with Peter. He would attend meetings at random, throw in questions like grenades – then leave early, not waiting for answers. No one knew his plans for his shares. The directors constantly complained amongst themselves – and sometimes to their colleagues – that they wish he would just sell them the business and go.

I asked one of the directors why Mr Worthing was hanging on. Her response stuck with me to this day. "Because," she replied, "at the moment he is Peter Worthing, chairman of Worthing and Leeds. The second he retires he'll just be Peter Worthing."

Understanding the motivation of all parties is key in succession planning.

Allow individuals to flourish

Not all employees will feel comfortable accepting the control handed to them. There may be several reasons for this – one may well simply be the adjustment required. And not everyone will believe that they really *are* being allowed a say. This will be especially likely in a company that has been run by a strong or domineering character.

Remember the pyramid. Business decisions need to be mapped against the flag. The employees need to know about the new ownership model. They need to know that they will be listened to, that their decisions will be implemented and not ignored. Only then will employees start to think more like business owners. And that means the current leaders need to make room and allow the employees to step up.

Stepping aside to allow others to take over is likely to mean a flatter decision-making structure, which encourages everyone to contribute. In this way some individuals will not only enjoy having a say but will positively flourish. And they might not necessarily be the people you might have predicted!

To quote Mike Brearley from *On Form* again:

> "Steep hierarchies and an atmosphere in which juniors should be seen and not heard are factors in the suppression of individuality."

Moving from a dominant boss to an eternal business means recognising, as well as dealing with, such challenges.

Thinking about the box

I remember hearing a story when studying for my economics degree about a company that made boxes of matches. A factory worker went to the board and told them he had an idea that would increase profits by 15%. If they paid him a large sum of money, he would give them the idea.

The board thought that if the factory worker could think of this idea, then surely they or their research department could think of it. This would mean they'd make the extra profits but not have to pay the man. So they said they'd get back to him.

Try as they might, however, the board could not find a change that would deliver such a dramatic increase in profits. They looked at compounds for the match-heads; new machinery; streamlined processes.

Eventually they admitted defeat and called the factory worker back in. They agreed to pay him if the results really were that dramatic. What, they asked him, was this brilliant idea.

The idea, said the man, is this: only put the sandpaper, on which the match is struck, on one side of the box.

The change did indeed deliver the increased profits, and the board paid the man his fee.

(Note: I suspect this story might be apocryphal, but it does highlight the importance of encouraging individuality.)

Getting employees to think like owners

It is important to keep focused on the objective. You want to fade away from the business, leaving it in the hands of your staff.

It is possible that the senior staff have a sense of entitlement that will grate with you. They may also think that they have skills and knowledge that you do not believe they possess – yet.

Dealing with employees can, at times, feel like having children. Your kids don't appreciate all the things you do for them. How could they? That's not their fault. You've been in their shoes, but they haven't been in yours. One day the kids grow up and have children of their own, and only then do they start to understand the sacrifices their parents made for them.

So, how to get employees to think more like business owners? Here are a few suggestions:

- Respect them. There's a good chance they *do* know things you don't.

- Listen to them. Find out their motivations. When there is an argument, the participants often end up realising that they all want the same end goal.

- Give them decision-making powers. Allow them to prove themselves – or learn something in the process.

- Give them information, and give them training to know what to do with that information.

Give them responsibility, specifically that will have an impact on other people. This could be getting involved in the recruitment process, for example. Trust is a two-way street, it is built up block by block by both sides at the same time. Want to trust your employees? Show them a little trust to get them started.

Letting go of accountability

For employees to be fully engaged in decision-making, they need to accept accountability as well as responsibility. Whereas many people can take responsibility, only one person can hold accountability for something at one time.

That means allowing the employees to make decisions that are wrong. Not just wrong in the opinion of the owner but actually poor decisions. It is through mistakes that we learn. In the words of author Douglas Adams:

> "A learning experience is one of those things that says, 'You know that thing you just did? Don't do that.'"

Of course, in order for one person to let go of accountability, another has to take hold. Accountability – and responsibility – must not be forgotten as decision-making is spread and employees given a voice. Exactly how it rearranges is for the employees (perhaps instigated by the leadership team) to decide.

Context is necessary

One business owner decided he wanted to include his employees in business decision-making. He had not made any firm decisions about the ownership or structure of the business, but had read a book about team building.

Several meetings were convened. At the first meeting the owner explained that the employees were going to have more of a say in the running of the business. The first meeting would be to consider how they might go about this and what areas they would like to consider first. The owner said it was important that he would not be involved as this might influence their thinking, and he wanted this to be a real open-minded exercise. He then left the meeting.

The team asked him to attend the fourth meeting. They announced that they had reached their first decision. They had decided that they should all get an increase to their holiday entitlement.

Reflecting on this exercise, the owner realised that he had not provided any context to the request, no long-term objectives, nor information about the business. In some ways it was hardly surprising that their first decision would be concerned with their own terms and conditions!

EMPLOYEES: THINK LIKE A BUSINESS OWNER

Business owners and employees think differently. Employees tend to make decisions on a micro level, based upon their immediate world: their own terms and conditions, or their role and surroundings. This is, after all, what people are paid for. They are not there to think about the strategic direction of the business – that is what others are paid for.

A business owner, on the other hand, needs to make decisions on a macro level, for the good of the business. In a small business this is often in addition to decisions relating to *their* role within the business.

In order for an owner to leave a business (whether it is sold or they retire), they need to have made themselves non-essential to the business. This requires the incoming team to think and act like business owners, to make or contribute towards macro business decisions.

And in an employee-owned business, all employees should be encouraged to think like business owners.

Making business decisions

Thinking like a business owner does not come naturally to many people. For example, discussion about business issues needs to be abstract – if someone points out that something in the business isn't working very well, taking it personally isn't going to help. Better to work out what is going wrong in the system and fix it. If it *is* a person not performing, do they have sufficient support, is training required?

Few people are born to be leaders. Most business owners found the role thrust upon them, without any training or experience. They learn, they adapt – and this is what employees who find themselves in an employee-owned business also need to do.

Adapting to demands

When I worked for a large pension company, my sales manager used to call me into his office in order to set me weekly targets. We would ask how many appointments I had made in the last week, to which I would always reply: "One less than I would have done had I not had to attend this meeting."

I would explain that I was not motivated by targets, so it didn't matter what he set for me. I would work as hard as I could and if I happened to beat a target, so be it. His targets simply did not motivate me.

A few years later I had set up my own business. After around nine months my credit card failed in the supermarket because I had reached the credit

> limit and I had to leave the shopping behind. When I got home I realised that I had targets now whether I liked it or not!

Ownership and control

One important point for employees to understand is that ownership does not mean control. An employee-owned business is not a democracy. Whilst the decision-making may be widened to harvest as many ideas as possible, it is likely that certain decisions will continue to be the responsibility of a small number of individuals, who are not necessarily elected to their posts.

An experiment in industrial democracy

The John Lewis Partnership refer to their business ownership structure as being "An experiment in industrial democracy". This democratic approach of allowing everyone to have a say leads to different business decisions. For example, if they are considering closing a shop, it is not because of the demands of outside shareholders since the Partnership does not have any.

The key expression is that the company is run on democratic principles. Whether it is a true democracy is something of a moot point. As a Waitrose board member, David Jones feels that he has been entrusted by Waitrose Partners to represent their views on their behalf, and that knowledge might not always change what he does, but may well affect how he does it.

This is perhaps best seen in the light of roles and responsibilities. The person best placed to make a decision about a technical issue is probably going to be the person who has the relevant technical qualifications – giving them both knowledge and experience. The person best placed to make a decision about the overall direction of the business is going to be one who has all the information available to them, plus experience of making such decisions.

This doesn't mean that each of those two employees can't have a say in each other's decision, but, ultimately the decision should be made by the person who is best placed to make it.

Accountability and responsibility

As already touched upon, an early topic for discussion should be the difference between accountability and responsibility. Responsibility can be shared by many people, however accountability for something can only be held by one person at a time. Consequently, responsibility can be delegated, accountability cannot.

Being responsible for something means that you take ownership of that thing happening. It involves discharging an obligation, making sure there is an outcome.

Being accountable for something means that you are *held to account* for the outcome. In a way, accountability is like souped-up responsibility – you are responsible for something happening but also answerable for it as well.

Accepting accountability is one of the key differences between thinking like an employee and thinking like a business owner.

One action to help employees to be more engaged and think like business owners might be to hold a group discussion on the differences between accountability and responsibility, giving examples within the business of each.

Dealing with the owner

In order for a business to become eternal, control must be devolved away from the current owner. Perhaps this might be managed over time, for the owner to fade away from the business, leaving it in the hands of the employees.

There is one key requirement for someone to feel that they are able to let go of control – they need to feel that someone else is going to be capable of taking that control from them. Sure, they need to let go – but someone else needs to have a good firm grip first.

This is not something that happens overnight. Respect is earned, and if both parties understand this basic principle, giving opportunities to earn trust and taking them when they are offered, slowly but surely the ground can shift.

What is extremely unlikely, however, is that an owner will, overnight, simply hand over control. There is a good chance that the owner has done things that the young employee simply cannot understand – and has scars from battles they don't even know about. This might be an unhelpful attitude, a blockage which is stopping the business from moving forward, but only empathy on both sides will enable this to be overcome.

So, how to get the owner to allow you to take more responsibility? Here are a few suggestions:

- Respect them. There's a good chance they do know things you don't.

- Listen to them. Find out their motivations. When there is an argument, participants often end up realising they all want the same end goal.

- If given decision-making powers, take it as an opportunity to prove yourself. And if it doesn't work out as you hoped, (visibly) use it as an opportunity to learn.

- Seek information. Read business books; learn how to read a set of accounts; find out what are the basic principles of marketing. Research the area of the business that interests you.

Most importantly, take responsibility and accountability when offered, and use it to show that you consider the impact of your actions and decisions on other people. Trust is a two-way street. You want your boss to trust you? Make them.

EMPLOYEES AND EMPLOYERS: TRUE COLLABORATION

An early reaction of some employees once they know that they are going to have to contribute to business decisions is to rub their hands with glee and think: 'At last, I can get my ideas actioned.'

It can therefore be a good idea to manage expectations. Employees need to know that they are going to be invited to contribute towards making decisions, but that does not mean they are going to be able to do everything their own way. That is not collaborative decision-making!

The important distinction to make here is that an employee-owned business is not a democracy. Employees are going to have a say in the running of the business, but this does not mean that every suggestion is going to be acted upon. Managing such expectations will have a significant effect on the discussions that take place and the decisions they lead to.

Dialogue not conversation

In the book *Not Knowing* by Steven D'Souza and Diana Renner, the authors highlight the subtle difference between conversation and dialogue. In a conversation, people exchange existing ideas, usually to promote their own point of view. They arrive at the conversation with pre-conceived ideas which they then defend or allow to be challenged. Generally when we are listening during a conversation we are preparing our response.

A dialogue, however, requires the participants to arrive with their views suspended. Listening becomes a process of understanding, rather than testing what the other person is saying against our existing views. A dialogue allows for opposite views to be aired and considered dispassionately and is more likely to result in decisions that are aligned to the flag.

The grab for power

If understanding each other's motivations is important for meaningful progress, the same can be said for understanding your own.

A reaction of certain individuals when it becomes clear that a succession plan is being considered, and control is being shared, can be a grab for power. This can destabilise the company, setting employees against each other, often to the annoyance of their colleagues, and delay real progress in establishing new decision-making procedures.

Such jockeying for position is unhelpful in almost every way. It is therefore worth attempting to anticipate and diffuse this power grab.

One thing needs to be made clear to all employees. In an eternal business, the control or 'power' is devolved. This is likely to require a shift in mindset of everyone involved.

In an eternal business, there should be little power *to* grab. Initially, this might not be popular with all employees, especially any that have been secretly hankering for the 'top job' for years. Sharing the ultimate objective therefore needs to be handled with sensitivity.

When announcing the change in ownership, the whole eternal business model should be explained. If the team know that decision-making is to be devolved, that the decision-making capabilities of the managing director or CEO are going to be considerably reduced, that the new boss is very much *not* going to be the same as the old boss, then the desire to step into those shoes should dissolve.

This barrier to devolving 'power' within a business may be exacerbated if the company is not 100% employee-owned. A company that is partly owned by a few shareholders that work within the business, and partly owned by a trust, needs to be very careful and transparent about its decision-making structures.

Avoiding a leadership vacuum

A marketing and advertising company had become owned by an employee ownership trust. Significant time was invested in communicating to employees how the new ownership and governance worked.

The founder believed that he had put an effective leadership team in place to succeed him. However, a few months after the shares were sold to the trust, the trustees received negative feedback from employees regarding the new CEO. The trustees eventually concluded that the CEO was not the right person to fill that role.

In particular, a leadership vacuum had developed which was leading a small number of employees to advocate themselves as the people who should be running the company.

The trustees of the employee ownership trust appointed a new CEO. They then invested time in explaining to employees that although it was vitally important to have their views on a range of matters, it was essential that management decisions be made by the leadership team.

Source: With thanks to Robert Postlethwaite of Postlethwaite's Solicitors Ltd

Eternal businesses do not suit everyone

One consequence of the move to an eternal business may be that some employees decide that it is not right for them, and leave. That's OK. It's not ideal, of course, but the nature of the company is changing. It is inevitable that not everyone will want to change with it.

Being part of an employee-owned business brings its own challenges. For example, employees may be expected to contribute to the business over and above their standard job description. There may well be a place for people who want to keep their head down and just do their job, especially in larger organisations, but the eternal business will, over time, attract people who subscribe to the flag. They are likely to be people who wish to make a contribution beyond their job description, no matter how small.

It is best for employees not to form opinions of what life might be like in the new-look business too soon. As the company transitions, it takes time to adjust, and both employees and departing owners need to allow each other plenty of space. There are enormous advantages from working for an eternal business that will replace the benefits that are perceived to have been lost.

Staying for a say in the direction of the company

Maya had been working for Lakeside Lowry Ltd for five years, and had been one of its brightest stars. She loved what the business stood for and felt she had a real say, and so accepted the fact that she was on a benefits package far below what she could get elsewhere. Although nothing had been said, her colleagues implied that she was a shoo-in for a directorship when the owner retired.

When the sale of the business to an employee ownership trust was announced, Maya became disillusioned. She finally accepted an invitation from a much larger competitor to be interviewed for an alternative position.

The managing director of the competitor who interviewed Maya explained the role they had in mind for her. The career path was mapped out, dependent upon hitting certain targets. He actually laughed when she told him her current earnings. He offered her a job there and then with potential earnings of more than double her current salary.

After considerable reflection, Maya turned down the job. The only attraction of the competitor company was the promise of making more money, which would entail working in a different, perhaps slightly less ethical, way. There was no clear sense of purpose of the business (other than making money). Nor did she feel that she would have any say in the direction of the company; she would just do her job.

Instead she chose to remain with her existing company and became central to making the business eternal.

Understanding some of these limitations is very important in bringing together the employees and leadership team looking to take over the running of the business with the owner. Once the move to employee ownership is announced, these issues will surface and need to be dealt with.

We'll now take a look at some possible decision-making structures, and consider how such a change might be introduced, bearing in mind the issues we have highlighted.

DECISION-MAKING STRUCTURES

A business which has decisions made by one individual might be dynamic and nimble. However, it is also more vulnerable if that individual makes a bad decision or leaves.

A business which has decisions made only by committees is likely to be cumbersome and slow to adapt to change.

The eternal business therefore needs a decision-making structure that is not dependent on a few individuals but instead uses a team-based approach. However, it also needs to avoid the potential for 'death by committee', a talking shop where decisions never get made because everyone needs to have their say.

It is important at the outset to emphasis that there is no 'right' decision-making structure. But there are effective principles to draw on – as well as the experience of others.

Some employee-owned companies have a traditional hierarchical structure. They tend to have a wide variety of skills and qualifications amongst their employees. Others, where the skills and qualifications of the employees are broadly similar, have a much flatter, cooperative-type structure. The structure that is right for your business will evolve.

Typical business structure

For small, owner-managed businesses, this is a typical structure:

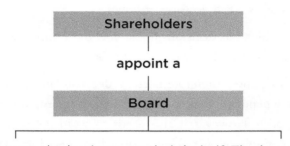

Shareholders

appoint a

Board

to run the business on their behalf. The board is made up of people both involved (directors) and not involved (non-executive directors) with the daily running of the business. The board appoints a

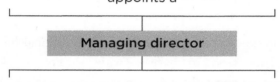

Managing director

who is accountable to the board for the day-to-day performance of the business. The managing director appoints a

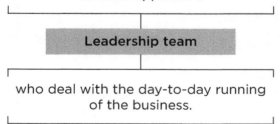

Leadership team

who deal with the day-to-day running of the business.

Depending on the size and nature of the business, this management strata can be wide or narrow. In a traditional, hierarchical business, this is often where decision-making stops.

The greater the dissemination of decision-making throughout the business, and the less decision-making is confined to a small number of people, the more likely the business is going to survive if a key employee leaves the company. And therefore the more likely the business can be eternal.

In an employee-owned business, the decision groups and the shareholders are effectively the same group of people – the employees. In this way the employees begin to become genuinely motivated to make good decisions as they directly affect the performance of the business which they own.

We therefore require a structure which will both contribute to the longevity of the business *and* engage employees.

The decision group structure

There are many ways of structuring decision-making. For example, focus groups (often called employee councils) which enable employees to have a voice directly to the board are common in larger businesses.

At Ovation we decided to set up decision-making groups in order that employees would be directly involved in making business decisions (this is, of course, easier in a smaller business).

We divided the various needs of the business into categories (marketing, finance, IT, social, etc). Employees were then invited to join at least one of the groups. We gave each group terms of reference, to make sure that all the decisions needed to be taken by the business were covered, and sensitive issues (such as certain HR issues) remained with the leadership team.

Our structure therefore evolved into this:

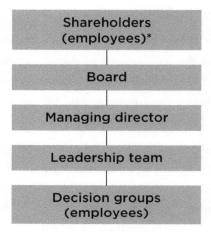

Noting that the employees are beneficial shareholders, as beneficiaries of the employee ownership trust.

The decision groups will be making or contributing towards real business decisions. The role of the leadership team is to corral the activity of these groups and deal with sensitive decisions. The role of the managing director is to ensure that the decisions being made are a) consistent with the strategy set by the board and b) consistent with the flag as set by the shareholders – who are the employees!

The board is appointed by the shareholders. And the shareholders are the employees!

This is, of course, just one possible structure for decision-making (and will constantly evolve). It does, however, demonstrate the circular nature of decision-making in an eternal business.

Project group structure

Another business uses a structure which involves retaining the hierarchical arrangement, but invites anyone to get involved in decision-making projects. If too many apply, then all the employees decide on the three or four to actually join the group. That project group then conducts the research and comes back to the team to present their proposals.

If too few people join the project (each project needs more than two) then it does not commence, as it has not attracted sufficient support.

After the project group has presented its proposals, those proposals *will* be implemented. The only way that someone who disagrees with a proposal can block it is if they can prove it will be damaging to the business – for example, financially – or if it is in conflict with the flag.

The advantage of this system is that anyone can get involved in a project, and everyone feels they have a real say in the direction of the company. The business that operates this system has around 25 employees.

Leadership – *The Catcher in the Rye*

If the company has strong decision-making throughout the organisation, the leadership team is able to see the bigger picture, whereas the decision-making groups will be focused on their narrower briefs.

The role of the owner, leadership team or executive is then likely to be akin to the 'catcher in the rye'.

In the novel *The Catcher in the Rye* by J. D. Salinger, the title refers to a poem which depicts children playing and running blindly through tall rye grass on the edge of a cliff. The narrator of the poem sees himself as standing just outside of the grass, catching any children who burst out of the rye towards the cliff.

In the same way the leadership team might see themselves as able to allow decision-making to flourish and innovate within the business, knowing that if any decision group is about to run off the cliff (perhaps defined as a decision that is not in keeping with the flag), it is able to step in and catch them.

Of course, knowing *when* to step in is something of a skill in itself. Not all interventions will be welcomed, and could be perceived in the early days as not being able to give up control. Each time the urge to step in manifests itself, it is worth asking whether this is really to prevent a decision akin to falling off a cliff, or because of a desire to retain control. Furthermore, if a poor decision is imminent, will it harm the business or could it lead to a learning opportunity?

In a business where the management structure is 'light touch', therefore, an intervention criteria will help provide clarity on where the control rests within the business.

Lack of hierarchy, higher honesty

Richard Elsner of Pivotal Moment Transitions Ltd spoke to a number of employee-owned businesses to find out how leadership might differ for them over traditional business models.

His conclusions were that leadership tends to be more devolved in employee-owned companies; that employees tend to have a greater sense of accountability; and that employee-owned businesses tend to be less hierarchical.

As a result, they tend to be characterised by high levels of honesty and greatly enhanced customer service.

How to find the right structure for your business

There are many ways in which staff can contribute to the decision-making of the business. For example, architectural practice Stride Treglown (with some 320 employees) has an employee forum. The members are elected and receive the minutes from the main board. They are then able to pass their remarks back to the main board as well as being able to raise any issues or concerns of their own.

A different approach has been taken by PES, which provides employee benefits and HR support to its own employees. They set up committees for each department in a similar way to the house structure in schools. Any person from any department can join different houses. They set targets which, when achieved, earn house points, and there is a prize for the house with most points at the end of 'term'. This system can deliver other benefits – for example, being a house captain can provide leadership experience for less-experienced employees. (For more, see: **www.wearepes.co.uk/hr-support/performance-management/reward**).

There are some innovative organisations that are not employee-owned, but which have put employees at the heart of decision-making in their businesses. Whilst rare, such companies do tend to thrive. (See *Reinventing Organizations* by Frederic Laloux, and Ricardo Semler's *Maverick*.)

The structure that is right for your business will evolve once the employees embrace the concept of the eternal business. The process should therefore be to:

1. inform the employees of the plan to become an eternal business

2. educate them on the issues that need to be worked through before the company can become employee-owned (the eternal pyramid)

3. encourage the employees to engage in the process of working out what structure is most going to suit them.

We will therefore look next at what can be done to create the best environment possible to allow employees to really understand their new role, and thereby evolve a decision-making infrastructure that will allow the existing owner to let go and enable the business to become eternal.

CREATING AN ENVIRONMENT TO ENCOURAGE EXCELLENT BUSINESS DECISIONS

Whether it is all the staff or a leadership team, there is a leap to be made for most employees from thinking like an employee to making decisions and thinking like a business owner.

There are actions that can generate leaps forward and allow the new decision-making structure to evolve. In this section we will look at a few of these.

Information flow

Sharing information enables employees to think like business owners. Good decisions can only be made if there is sufficient information to provide context and meaning to the issue at hand.

This includes sharing what might previously have been thought of as being sensitive information.

The most notable example of this is financial information. Many owners whose businesses have become employee-owned report that sharing financial information *in a meaningful way* (thereby sharing knowledge) with employees resulted in the biggest step change in employee engagement.

When information energises employees

In Ovation I tended to keep financial information close to my chest. I would share some of the headline figures with the staff on an irregular basis, or when specifically requested to. One employee once enquired how much it costed for us to be regulated by the government in order to be allowed to give advice (the staff were astounded to a degree that, in turn, greatly surprised me).

Only in the few years preceding our move to be an employee-owned company did I begin to share more financial information, allowing one other member of staff to see the accounts. He went on to become our finance director.

It was to my great surprise, therefore, that the biggest leap forward in the team's understanding of what it meant to think more like business owners came the day that I allowed them to see the accounts.

> The finance director took everyone through the accounts and our forecasting, explaining the assumptions and implications of certain changes, and answered any questions. The effect was transformative. Finally, the employees understood the pressures on the business; what we were aiming to achieve and why we had chosen those targets; the financial strength of the business; and the potential profits (which they would get to share in).
>
> One employee even commented that he had no idea how well I had been running the business!

Information flow to employees is key in an eternal business. However, it is important to give consideration to *how* the information is shared. Simply sending out a full set of accounts to every employee will not make them more informed.

Sharing **meaningful information** in an educational and informative way will not only provide employees with knowledge to inform their input on decisions, but it will also show that the company is truly committed to employee engagement.

Personality profiling

Another huge step-change in employees moving towards making good business decisions can be personality profiling. Having a variety of different personality types in a team can be positive, but many employees will not be used to having their voice heard, may be shy, or worried about putting their necks out. Others may grab the opportunity to finally have their say and end up dominating.

Personality profiling within a group – including sharing each other's results with each other – enables the team to understand *why* people behave like they do. That, for instance, some people like to make instant decisions whereas others need time to think before they offer an opinion. That some become overbearing in conflict, others shut down and may have a tendency to not respect decisions made at such times.

By understanding how each other works (and how we ourselves react in conflict), teams are better placed to relate to each other in ways that were far more productive, and thereby begin to make better collaborative decisions.

Understanding the process

One extension of this idea is to share information about the decision-making process itself. One company provides employees with a booklet about their decision-making processes. It outlines the decision-making structure within the business, where decisions are made, how and by whom. It also includes a summary of the statement of principles of the business, in order that decisions may be tested against it.

One extra gain from this might be to nip in the bud the 'power grab', by ensuring everyone understands that control is being passed from the current owner to the employees as a whole, via the chosen decision-making structure.

Mapping to the flag

As we have seen above, the role of the leadership team in an eternal business might be to ensure that decisions are aligned both with the current strategic plan for the business and with the flag.

As was stressed in chapter 3, the clearer the sense of purpose of the business, the more likely good business decisions will be mapped in accordance with the flag. This includes sharing the flag with the team, and making sure everyone understands what it means.

Show what success might look like

As part of deciding to be employee-owned first, but actioning it last, it can be helpful to make it clear what such a business might look like; what might actually happen within such a business.

For example, one characteristic of an eternal business is transparency. This might mean not only the sharing of company financial information with the employees, but also the sharing of employee remuneration with each other.

Another example might be the role of the current boss. One mark of success for an eternal business is for decision-making to be devolved. In this case, what will the role of the current boss be in the future? If it is to be the *Catcher in the Rye*-type role, then paint this as a possibility early on. Indeed, why not even get the employees to decide on the role of the boss?

When employees determine the role of the boss

Matt Tipping founded Double Europe and was its creative heart. As managing director he arranged an awayday for him and the team to talk about how they made decisions.

Some time in the afternoon, Matt told his team that he was going to take a walk. In his absence he wanted them to discuss what *his* role in the business was to be in the future. He would do whatever they asked of him. If they thought his skills would best help the business by making the tea or answering the telephones, that's what he would do.

He came back from his walk after 40 minutes, entered the room, sat down, and asked if they had reached a decision. They confirmed they had.

"OK, then," he said, "what do you want me to do in the business?"

"Well," his team replied. "We would like you to interfere less – and mentor more."

Replacing the front person

As decision-making gets more and more devolved, and the owner starts the process of becoming less of a figurehead (or maybe leaving entirely), it is worth considering how to replace the gravitas that might have been provided by the presence of the founder or visionary.

Sometimes, when a client wants to make a complaint, or a new client is considering signing up, or an important existing client wants to feel loved, a meeting with the founder or owner can make a real difference. Depending on how much of the founder's personality and reputation can be found in what the business produces, it may therefore be helpful to keep them on for a while, perhaps in an ambassadorial role.

Do, however, be very clear over their role within the business.

Feedback

We have already cited information flow as being essential to employee engagement and excellent decision-making structures evolving. Well, this information flow needs to go both ways.

If management receive information that something is not working, how should they respond?

Logic suggests that such information is the very information management need in order to make improvements. Too often, however, this feedback is received as criticism, to be stifled in case it makes management look bad.

Many companies and organisations will recognise this sort of reaction to feedback, where input from staff is at best not sought, at worst ignored. The result is the opposite of what we wish to achieve. Employees will be disengaged, as they do not believe their voice is being listened to.

Inviting ideas and contributions, encouraging employees to be part of the decision-making process, is crucial, but it needs to be genuine.

The opposite of yet another survey

Two surgeons from Bristol, Andy Hollowood and Anne Frampton, wanted to find out what staff at all levels within the hospitals in their area were thinking. They did not, however, want to take yet another staff survey, which would give a snapshot at a particular point in time. Instead they wanted real-time feedback.

They were aware of the 'happy/sad' approach, offering customers a choice of two feedback buttons on the way out of a shop. They liked the concept, but wanted more – a real channel of communication between staff and management, in real time.

They created the Happy App to solve this problem. Available on all devices and set up in every ward, the Happy App enables staff to bash out a comment virtually on the run. These comments can be viewed instantly by managers, who have various options. They can simply take note of a comment, building multiple comments into a picture of what is actually happening. If it is a specific issue they can take action. If a suggestion, it can be taken onboard.

It's fair to say that certain managers were nervous of using the Happy App. Already overworked, the last thing they wanted was a torrent of complaints from staff who were themselves overworked and stressed. Slowly, however, various departments agreed to trial the app.

The first result that surprised and delighted Andy and Anne was that the split of comments between those that were pointing out a problem or issue, and those that were positive feedback, was around 50:50. Lots of comments were simply along the lines of: "I just want to say what a fantastic team we are, I am so proud of my colleagues".

Another feature was that the cries for help could be acted upon. More than once a crisis on a ward could be dealt with immediately and, on one occasion, this may even have saved the life of a desperate member of staff who was considering taking her own life.

As well as the potential for instant intervention, the responses built into trends in a very short space of time. This allowed managers to not only deal with issues as they arose but then take more systemic action as pictures emerged of what was needed.

The Happy App has now been adopted not only by many other health trusts, but other organisations outside the health sector as well.

Making informed business decisions

One interesting question to debate as the decision-making structure evolves is the extent to which members of a decision-making team need to be knowledgeable about the subject to which they are contributing. Will anyone be allowed to join any decision or project group? And if so, will they be required to become knowledgeable on that subject?

The objective is to make decisions that are best for the business. There can be a danger that someone who knows little about a subject is more likely to vote subjectively, based upon personal preference and values, rather than objectively, based upon knowledge.

When disagreements occur, it is generally due to a lack of information. Sometimes that information will be impossible to come by (for example, the impact of a particular decision). However, one outcome from disagreements will often be to obtain additional knowledge. If the people who are contributing towards the decision are knowledgeable in that subject in the first place, disagreements must surely be less likely to happen.

The extent to which knowledge is part of decision-making groups is worth discussing at an early stage.

CONCLUSION

Collaborative decision-making and efficient teams do not appear overnight. They take time, dedication to the cause, and an understanding of the objective from *all* parties. It requires owners to let go of control while employees grab hold. It needs a clear flag against which decisions can be judged.

Decision-making structures within employee-owned businesses evolve. Existing structures and councils need testing to see whether they are discussing real business issues, or just their own working conditions. Effective decision-making needs to be in place long before the actual act of selling to the employee ownership trust, in order that the owner will feel that their company – and their earn-out! – will be in safe hands.

The result will be a company with a wide knowledge base that contributes towards decisions. There will be a shared sense of purpose and achievement amongst employees. And those employees will feel engaged and motivated because they have a genuine say in the running of the business.

The next part of building our eternal pyramid is to retain our focus on the employees, and consider how else we can make them motivated and engaged.

Chapter 5

ENGAGED EMPLOYEES

INTRODUCTION

I t has long been acknowledged that a business *is* its employees. But how many businesses really put their employees at its heart?

Sure, we talk a good game. But do we really understand what motivates employees? Do we really create an environment in which they can not only thrive professionally, but also personally?

Having happy and motivated employees doesn't just mean paying for a Christmas party, or addressing them once a year by way of the annual report. For a business to transition control away from the existing owner, employees need to be motivated for both themselves *and* the business to succeed.

And in order for this to happen, they need to understand what success would look like. Again, both for themselves *and* for the business.

In the previous chapter we talked about sharing information about business performance with

ENGAGED EMPLOYEES

employees. Now we'll look at how to create clarity over the future for the employees themselves.

In this chapter we will therefore look at: what motivates people at work; creating a financial plan to provide employees with a clear path to identifiable objectives; how to construct a career plan for employees; how the career and financial plan work together to help create the eternal business.

Author's note: *This chapter is not intended to give you all that you need to know about HR or, for that matter, financial planning. There are many, many books on these subjects, and I have suggested a few in the bibliography. Instead, this chapter focuses on engaging employees within an eternal business by creating a pathway both personally and within the business.*

There are many other important aspects of engaging employees which are common to all businesses. However, clarifying and highlighting the meaningful nature of the employment is especially pertinent in an eternal business, in a business where control moves from the existing owner to the employees. The career and financial plan is therefore of particular relevance to an employee-owned business, and will supplement other employee engagement programmes and changes in organisational culture that may need to take place.

OVERVIEW: COMBINING PERSONAL AND PROFESSIONAL

With clarity of the sense of purpose of the business via the flag, and involvement in decision-making, working within an eternal business is likely to feel different from working for a traditional business. It is likely to be far more fulfilling.

In order to assist owners in the transition of control to the employees, the employees need to be truly committed to the success of the business. The way to achieve this is by giving employees clarity over the future – both personally and professionally.

Loyalty develops when there is clarity over the future. Given that we spend most of our time at work, and that what we earn shapes both our present and our future lives, that clarity can come from bridging what we do at work with what we do outside of work.

A business with employees who are happy and engaged with the performance of the business must surely have an increased chance of succeeding. But what if those employees were also able to see how their life goals could be achieved through their job? That every time they walked through the door to work they knew what they needed to do to achieve all that they wanted from life? Surely then the business would have a real chance of thriving for the long term: of being eternal.

In this section, therefore, we will look at how to truly motivate employees. This will involve linking what they do during the working day, and the resultant performance of the company, to their own life goals. It will show the benefits of a combined **career** and **financial** plan.

Learning how to get the future you want

Bob Welsh used to be a skipper. He had sailed the Atlantic many times, but had changed career to become a solicitor. He still loved boats, however, and held a longstanding dream that when he retired he would buy a Cornish Crabber - a type of sailing boat. He would live on the boat and sail it around the south coast of England.

Although retirement was 20 years away, Bob constructed a financial plan. He spoke with his employer and they agreed together what Bob might expect by way of pay rises in the event of certain staging posts, such as obtaining qualifications. They were also able to give an indication of what his possible profit-share might be over the coming years. Bob was able to include both these in his financial plan.

As a result, Bob had a plan that showed him what he had to do to be able to afford to purchase his longed-for Cornish Crabber boat in 20 years' time, and possibly a few years sooner if things went better than expected. Every time he arrived at work, he knew what he needed to do to get the future that he wanted.

How would a motivated team behave?

One way of measuring when a team has truly formed would be whether each member of the team knows and values the contribution of each other member. Might such a team be comfortable knowing each other's salaries? This would demonstrate that everyone knows and is comfortable with the contribution to the business of everyone else.

Let's take this one step further. Imagine that not only do all staff know each other's salaries, but that the end of the year arrives and there are profits to be shared out. Suppose the employees in a department are told the size of the total bonus pot, and that they needed to go into a room and agree amongst each other how it was to be shared.

Now imagine them coming out smiling! THAT would be a measure of success, would it not?

Or how about if there are **no** profits to be shared out. Now, instead of simply being given the news by management, employees get involved in making tough decisions. They get to share in the pride of laying the foundations for something amazing.

Building something amazing by sacrificing together

The National Self Build and Renovation Centre became an employee-owned business when it was struggling. Selling to an employee ownership trust was a way for the employees to step in to save a business that they felt passionately about.

After two years of hard work, the company first broke even, and then made a profit. Just before Christmas the managing director, Harvey Fremlin, gathered the team to tell them the good news.

He suggested that they were faced with a dilemma. After all their hard work and commitment, they would now be able to take the profits and each receive a share. This would only be a fair reward.

There was, however, another possibility. The team could decide not to take the bonus, and instead

> reinvest the profits into the business to further strengthen the company. He asked the team what did they want to do.
>
> The decision to reinvest in the business was unanimous. Buoyed by this additional cash, the company continued its recovery and is now flourishing.

The employee financial plan

At the beginning of this process of making a business eternal, we said that the first step was for the owner to work out how much they need to achieve what they want in life. Well, now it's time to apply that same principle to the employees.

Studies have shown that financial wellbeing comes from having **a clear path to identifiable objectives** (see *The Financial Wellbeing Book* for more). This means that creating a financial plan comes in two distinct stages:

Step 1: Having clarity over personal objectives.

Step 2: Creating a financial path to achieve those objectives.

It also means having clarity over your career, in terms of both the role and the financial compensation, in order to provide that information to feed into the financial plan.

It's all connected!

Clarity over personal objectives

This first step in financial planning is to get clarity over what an ideal (and achievable) future might look like.

The financial plan should establish some objectives for a happy life. These don't have to be clearly defined goals. Indeed, working towards absolute goals which aren't allowed to be altered can cause its own problems. (For more on the danger of focusing too heavily on goals, read 'Chapter 4: Goal Crazy' of *The Antidote* by Oliver Burkeman.) A financial plan just needs to start with a vague idea of what a happy future might look like.

For some this may be very clear, for others less so. The process of identifying objectives should answer questions such as:

- How much is enough?

- How will you know when the time has come to stop work?

- If you had financial freedom, what would you spend your time doing?

The answers to these and similar questions will help employees understand why it is that they come to work over and above the basic need to pay the bills.

There will be very different outcomes for different people. Some examples of answers to the 'financial freedom' question might include:

- retiring to pursue other interests

- never retiring (or possibly being afraid of retiring)

- work less when the children are young then throw themselves into the job when the kids leave home

- work part time at some point to be able to care/pursue a hobby or education

- home educate children.

Employees may find it difficult to share these aspirations with their boss. However, if employees *were* able to be candid about their aspirations, if it was recognised that everyone in the company was working towards personal goals in life, their career and personal plans would stand more chance of becoming aligned – to the benefit of both the individual and the business.

Creating a financial path to achieving those objectives

The next step in the financial plan is to plot a financial path to that chosen future. This could be in the form of a simple spreadsheet or a cash flow forecast. Employees could do this themselves or use the services of a financial planner (or use a tool such as *The Financial Wellbeing Book*).

The forecast will take into account current assets, and current and future income and expenditure, to project the financial position at a future age, perhaps 100. This process will lead to one of two possible outcomes:

- There *is* money left at the end. This means the chosen future is affordable. In fact, some changes might be possible, such as spending more now, or retiring earlier.

- There is *no* money left at the end. This means the chosen future is not affordable. This will require changes, such as spending less now and saving more, or retiring later.

Either outcome will lead to a refinement of the plan. This will result in a circular process, with each circuit bringing clarity.

When initially working out what their chosen future might look like, most people tend to make assumptions based on their current circumstances. The financial planning process should encourage one to dream a little, to test different futures to see what might be possible.

This is, of course, the process that started the business owner on shaping what they wanted from their business. Well, this same process should have a similar effect on employees.

Once the forecast of the future starts to take shape, this will lead people to start making a few decisions about their future. And one very important area of their lives that they will start to think about is how much money they need for their future, how much time they spend doing things they enjoy, how fulfilled they are, and so on. In other words, they will begin to focus on their careers.

THE CAREER PLAN

Now each employee has a meaningful financial plan, providing clarity over what the future might look like. Next, let's look at how to provide clarity over their career.

Objective of a career plan

The purpose of a career plan is to provide clarity over the future for an employee. This plan has two potential outcomes:

- to produce engaged employees
- to ensure that everyone is working to common objectives.

Remember that each side of the eternal pyramid leans on the others, and this is another example. The career plan is a way of ensuring employees are aligned to the common purpose of the business.

The components that make up happy staff

As Daniel H. Pink points out in *Drive*, as the nature of our work has changed from rote to solution-finding, so what motivates the modern employee has changed from the carrot of financial reward or the punishment of losing one's job, to a sense of purpose and meaning.

Employee happiness can be broken down into five key areas:[2]

- job understanding, i.e. purpose
- performance
- succession planning
- training
- development.

Let's look at each of these in a bit more detail.

---

2   See the Bibliography for more information on how this list was compiled.

Job understanding:

What does the organisation want to achieve (the flag)?

How does my role contribute towards the flag?

Hierarchies

Specialists or generalists

Build 'levels' within job families (by skills/experience/competences)

Performance:

Objective setting

Reviewing performance

Personal development planning

Reward for performance

Succession planning:

What do you need and when for each role

Training:

Skills to do the current role

Skills to stimulate

Development:

Aim for next role

Gap analysis – between current and next job

Plan to fill that gap – training of skills, experience, competence training/exposure

Qualifications

Mentoring and coaching

A word about structure

We have already established that to build an eternal business we need to move control from the owner to the employees. We have established that this includes developing collaborative decision-making structures.

Such decision-making will benefit if each employee has clarity over the roles performed by others in the organisation. It therefore follows that the more involvement the team have in designing the various levels of an organisation structure, the better they will understand the skills and qualifications required for each level.

This will bring context and therefore greater understanding to the career plan; enable appreciation of the skills and talents of others; and lead to the sort of openness that will eventually allow for all staff to know and understand the roles – and remuneration – of their peers.

Putting career plan theory into practice

The first part of the process is to understand the current roles and responsibilities for each employee using the above criteria. The next stage is to create a plan which fills in the gaps.

The career plan can be ambitious regarding end objectives if appropriate for the employee, but it is important to create the plan with one development stage at a time. Things change all the time, and anything more than 12 months away should be flexible.

The plan can, however, stretch into the future, and thereby produce potential earnings and profit-share for insertion into the financial plan. As long as it is understood by all parties that anything over 12 months is guesswork, it will at least enable the employee to plot a potential financial future. (For more on this, see *Traction* by Gino Wickman.)

The steps would include the following:

- review current performance and discuss personal aspirations

- talk through current role and aspirations within the context of the organisational structure

- agree a personal development plan to show what needs to happen next

- think about a general development plan which applies to the whole team to fulfil core needs (examples might include how to read financial accounts or what is marketing)

- review regularly (whatever timing works best for the person – as we are all different – but at least every six months) to monitor progress, discuss what happens next, manage any expectations and agree next steps.

Looking up

Nucleus is not an employee-owned business, but it does have some forward-looking ideas.

Like an eternal business, it has a visions and values statement. When employees go through its performance review procedure, performance is not compared with a list of targets set for them by someone else.

Instead, employees are asked to discuss what they have done in their work that is aligned to the vision and values of the business.

> The result is that rather than focusing on their own little part of the business, they are encouraged to look up every half year and consider the business in its wider context.

There is a plan; then again there is a *plan*

As Claire James at Pivotal Moment puts it:

"The actual nature of the career plan (and, for that matter, the financial plan) should be relatively fluid. It is very easy for a manager who is motivated by having a clear path, with staging posts and key performance indicators, to assume that this will motivate others.

"This is not always the case. Some may want looser plans; some may not be able to see the future clearly – or only in general terms; some may want to only plan for the immediate future; some may want to be supported in having multiple options open to them.

"The important thing is for the company to have systems that allow the individual to craft the *process* of planning in a way that suits them, as well as the desired format of the plan that emerges."

Managing expectations within an eternal business

As we know, each side of the eternal pyramid affects the others. Collaborative decision-making will benefit from encouraging employees to be involved in areas that are not directly linked to their role. For example, a member of the HR team might join a marketing group.

Another example might be if one of the accounts team shines, but the business is unlikely to be big enough to warrant a full-time finance director. If this is their goal, the company can still help them grow, and prepare them for a move to finance director with another company. This will be positive for the brand (both external and internal). Furthermore, that individual may well return if the company *does* grow sufficiently to meet their aspirations.

It might at first seem counterintuitive for a business to prepare employees to move elsewhere: surely, though, it is better for people to be happy in their roles than frustrated at the lack of opportunity. It's also better for the business to prepare for employees that are leaving, rather than keeping aspirations quiet, resulting in unpleasant surprises for the business.

Within the core team this is unlikely to be an issue, but there may not be enough 'bigger' jobs to satisfy everyone. Not everyone wants (or can be) the top dog. Instead there should be a focus on being (for example) the very best administrator – which should be recognised and rewarded.

The career plan informing the financial plan

There are three ways in which career progression can result in financial rewards:

- increases in base salary

- bonuses and/or commission

- profit-share.

There are other benefits that can be awarded – for example, extra holidays and other rewards. These can be greatly appreciated, can enhance employee happiness and be less costly for the company. Rather than go into a full employee benefits programme, however, we will focus on the above three as they are the ones that can be plugged into the personal financial plan.

In an employee-owned business, the profit-share is the least flexible, as it can typically only be varied by reference to hours worked; length of service; and salary (see the next chapter for more on this).

The old saying has it that form is temporary but class is permanent. And so it goes with bonuses and salary. A bonus can be awarded based upon performance and is a one-off. An increase in salary lasts forever. Consequently they are awarded for different types of activity – temporary (winning a particular contract) or permanent (obtaining qualifications).

THE COMBINED CAREER AND FINANCIAL PLAN

The financial plan and the career plan can now inform each other. The two parts to the plan inform each other. Adding something to the career plan may affect the financial plan, and vice versa.

The career plan should produce numbers, in terms of potential salary increases and bonuses. It will also provide the potential profit-share. Each of these can be factored into the financial plan.

The financial plan begins with the question 'What makes me happy?' However, this needs to be informed by a dose of realism – with a second question: 'Can I afford it?'

The career plan can therefore provide answers to questions such as 'What is achievable?'. Combine these two questions, and the clear path to identifiable objectives will emerge.

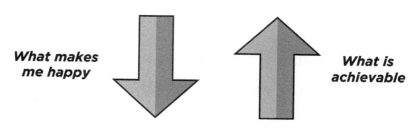

FINANCIAL PLAN

What makes me happy

What is achievable

CAREER PLAN

A common concept is the 'work/life balance'. The combined career and financial plan provides a forecast of that principle. Both parts of the equation should work together, resulting in this employment leading to a happy and fulfilled life.

Financial plan	Career plan
What do I want to achieve in life?	What do I want to achieve in my career?
What do I need financially to achieve what I want in life?	What do I need to achieve in my career?
Am I on track to achieve what I want in life?	Is my career on track to meet my financial plan?
How might taking a career break impact on my financial plan?	How might taking a career break impact my future career?
Are there any changes I would like to make in my life (e.g. being home to read a story to the kids)?	Are there any changes I could make to how I work (e.g. delegating to reduce hours worked)?
Do I need to earn more?	What would my role look like if I earned more?
Could I manage on earning less?	What would my role look like if I earned less?
Am I happy with my financial plan?	Am I happy with my career plan?

ADVANTAGES TO THE BUSINESS

The objective of the career and financial plan is to create employees who arrive at work knowing what they have to do to get the future they want. This will help create engaged employees.

There are other ways in which the career and financial plan informs the other sides of the eternal pyramid. For example, roles will have clear alignment with the principles of the business as espoused by the flag; employees with development plans that reflect their contribution to decision-making.

Two-way employee communication

Engaged employees also provide advantages for business planning. Too often businesses have a 'them and us' mentality. A person who is unhappy in their job and is looking around for a change will typically not tell their boss until they hand in their resignation letter.

As a boss of many years, I always found this frustrating. If someone had expressed their unhappiness to me earlier, we might have been able to do something about it.

Leaving the company is only one solution to dissatisfaction. A boss can only find solutions to problems that they know about. Only finding out when an employee hands in their notice is incredibly frustrating; the transparency of an eternal business should limit this.

Of course, the counter argument is that the boss should be more aware of the issues. Whilst that is undoubtedly often true, we have to be realistic. As I used to say to our employees, I don't tell my *wife* that I love her often enough, let alone you lot!

Creating a career plan that is regularly reviewed will ensure that there is more open communication.

Of course, it could be that the dissatisfaction is not something that can be solved by staying. Perhaps someone just wants a career change, or has been offered another job that the current company simply cannot match. Having open communication would mean airing this at an early stage. It might even be that the current employer could help the employee find their next job, and at the same time start to plan for a replacement.

Businesses don't like surprises

It will be obvious why these financial plans should be confidential. I'm not going to suggest they should not be, but let's just imagine what might happen if they were not. How would a culture of a business be different if the contents of what we want our future to look like were to be shared with our employers?

As a general rule, businesses don't like surprises. Planning for the future is much easier if all eventualities are known in advance. This is, of course, impossible, but the fewer imponderables, the easier the planning. And this is particularly relevant when it comes to employees.

For example, an employer cannot (and should not) ask a 28-year-old person if they have plans to have children. That is entirely right and proper due to the potential for discrimination.

Just imagine, however, if that conversation *was* allowed to take place, in an open-minded and mature environment, how it *could* work:

Employee: "I wanted to let you know that I want to have children in the next three years or so."

Employer: "OK, thanks for letting me know. It's probably a little early to know such things, but do you think you'll return to work?"

Employee: "I'd really love to, although I think I need to be realistic that I might not be able to do full time, from what others have said to me."

Employer: "OK, so we've got three years to plan for you being away for six months, then returning part time."

Such openness would allow both employee and employer to plan properly for the future. Wouldn't this be better for everyone?

CONCLUSION

Employees who arrive at work knowing what they need to do in order to secure the life that they want are far more likely to become engaged with the business.

This is particularly true for an eternal business, as the employees are also contributing towards business decisions.

We now have a business which has a clear sense of purpose that is shared and understood by employees and customers alike; a decision-making process to engage the employees; and employees with clarity over what the business can do for them in return.

The final stage is an ownership structure which will reward the employees; enable the existing owner to hand control over to the employees; and enable the existing owner to exit from the business.

Chapter 6

OWNERSHIP: A STRUCTURE FOR ALL

INTRODUCTION

Recap

Let us recap what we are looking to achieve from our company structure. Firstly, we want to provide an owner with an answer to the question of 'what next?' Secondly, we want to de-risk the business in order to maximise the likelihood of payments being made to the owner after ownership has passed to others. Thirdly, we want to provide clarity over the future for employees either worried about what might happen if the business is sold, or who want to get more involved with the business.

And in order to create an eternal business, we have identified that we need to:

- create a happy place to work, with inspired and engaged employees

- create a business where employees have a say in the running of the business, with clarity over what is expected of them and how they can contribute

- create a business with a focus on long-term sustainable profit

- take the focus away from the idea of a capital event such as the sale of the shares.

We have looked at three sides of the eternal pyramid – the three areas to particularly focus on to create an eternal business. The final side is a company structure that will bring everything together, to enable all four sides to lean on each other. The ownership structure needs to support the flag; give meaning to collaborative decision-making; provide potential rewards to plug into career and financial plans so as to create employee engagement.

In addition, our chosen ownership model should:

- allow the owner to release value from the business

- provide the owner with the option of an ongoing income from the business

- provide the owner with the option of an ongoing role in the business (a sense of purpose)

- enable the employees to benefit from the performance of the business

- allow the future of the business to be influenced by the employees

- ensure the clients of the business continue to be cared for.

In this chapter we will first look at different business structures, leading to the conclusion that our eternal business will be indirectly owned. In part 2 we will consider the business which is controlled by a trust for the benefit of the employees. Finally, in part 3, we will consider some of the issues companies face when moving from direct to indirect ownership.

OWNERSHIP

A brief note to anyone who has turned straight to this section

If you have jumped straight to this section – hi! This is arguably the most interesting section of the book, as it brings everything together. Business owners in particular might be tempted to start here, perhaps before handing the book to employees to read the rest.

But please – **don't** go taking any action on this chapter alone. Business owners, you need to have done some financial planning, and to get the business ready to live without you. If you like the idea of employee ownership, how you inform your employees needs to be handled with some sensitivity. Employees, the business needs to be structured so that it can thrive without the current owners, and that might take longer than you think.

In short, by all means read this chapter first. In fact, I'd say that's a really good idea! However, you should act upon it last.

The ownership structure should be decided first because it is key that employees know that there is going to be a change in the ownership of the business. This brings meaning to the other changes they will be asked to get involved with.

This involves obtaining an early understanding of the implications of moving to an employee-owned business. It doesn't necessarily mean making a decision on which precise structure is to be used. This will require a great deal of consideration in terms of both the implications for current owners and for new owners/employees.

The business should only be handed over to the employees when it is truly in a shape that means it is ready for the change; when the employees are in a position to accept the new responsibilities. This means only when the other three sides of the eternal pyramid have been completed.

For the owner there is a particular reason for this.

The payment for sale of the business is likely to come from future profits. In other words the owner will be paid by a business that the owner no longer controls.

This means that the business needs to be made eternal – to be de-risked – for the owner to feel *able* to relinquish control.

PART 1: BUSINESS STRUCTURES

As will have become clear by now, the company best suited to becoming an eternal business is one that is employee-owned. In part 2 we will look at what this means in depth, but first let's take a moment to consider the usual routes for owners to exit their businesses.

We touched on this in chapter 1 where we looked at traditional succession-planning models. We'll look at those options a bit more deeply and consider what the motivations might be for the various parties, before explaining why they are not right for a business that wishes to become eternal.

Direct ownership – buyouts

In simple terms, there are two ways that the shares of a business can be owned: directly by one or more individuals; or indirectly, perhaps by a trust.

Succession planning by direct ownership, through one of a number of methods, involves one person (or a group of people) buying the shares in the company from another person (or group of people).

The methods are many. MBOs (management buyouts), BIMBOs (buy-in management buyout), VIMBOs (vendor-initiated man... oh, you get the idea). The acronyms are seemingly endless.

There is a fundamental issue with each of these traditional routes which works against a business becoming eternal. None of these solve the problems that the owner faces in exiting their business. They merely hand those problems over to others.

The owner wants to get their value out of the business. A group of people (usually referred to as the 'management team') raises the money to buy out the owner. And now the management team has the problem of how to get *their* value out of the business one day. The obsession with value, and the problem of realising that value, simply continues.

In an eternal business the notion of value is removed.

The obsession with value

By definition, an eternal business is one that is not going to be sold. If this is the case, what purpose does valuing a business serve?

A business is typically valued by reference to the profits that it can generate. Take a business that is generating £100k of profits each year. Let us suppose that this values the business at £1m. Ten times profits or, to put it another way, the purchaser gets 10% p.a. return on their money. This means someone is willing to pay £1m in order to receive £100k back each year, ad infinitum.

One day, that person will want their £1m back. They will swap places with someone who is willing to give them £1m for £100k p.a. Perhaps for personal reasons, perhaps they need the capital. Maybe they want to reduce the risk of their investments.

Suppose, however, that the business is now making £200k profits each year. If 10% is still seen as a good return, then someone will pay them £2m to swap places – to receive that ongoing income.

Sometimes the new owners don't do so well, and the profits go down. Sometimes the company goes bust, and the £1m becomes nothing.

Everyone is trying to get their hands on the profits and is willing to pay good money for it.

What are the effects of this obsession with the value of the business? And at what point does this cycle stop?

M&A or A&E?

The cycle of mergers and acquisitions (M&A) creates an environment which is not necessarily to the best advantage of the customer. The world is littered with companies which have been bought from the founder(s) by a management team who were excited and confident in the new direction they wanted to take the business, only for their inexperience to result in the company failing.

On the flip-side, there have been many highly successful management buyouts, which have resulted in management selling on at a later date and becoming hugely rich in the process. There are also examples of management teams deliberately reducing the value of a business before taking it over, meaning they pay a low price and sell for a high price. (For example, see: **dealbook.nytimes.**

com/2013/02/05/reasons-to-be-suspicious-of-management-led-buyouts.)

Ultimately, what is everyone fighting over? The regular distribution of profits.

The game of corporate finance: offer price versus money received

There is also an issue with how business owners perceive the value of their businesses. Something that we already own, or that has personal meaning us, has a different value to us than it might do to other people.

The endowment effect in action

Economist Richard Thaler uses the expression the 'endowment effect' to describe how we tend to value something more highly if we already own it than if we do not.

Researchers gave one half of a group of students a coffee cup and asked them to come up with a value. The other half, who were not given the cup, were also asked to come up with a value. The group who owned the cup said they were unwilling to sell it for less than $5.25; the group who did not own the cup said they wouldn't want to pay more than $2.75.

Source: **bigthink.com/insights-of-genius/rethinking-the-endowment-effect-how-ownership-effects-our-valuations gave**

A business owner who has started a business, who has toiled day and night and made financial sacrifices, is often going to value their business higher than an accountant or potential purchaser. This gap between perceived value and actual value can be exploited by large companies when acquiring small businesses. This is how the game is played:

Step 1: The business owner has an expectation of what their business might be worth. This could come from articles in the trade press, or perhaps what their peers report they were offered.

Step 2: Another business, perhaps a large corporate, comes along and makes an offer. There is an amount promised upfront, an amount after one year, a final payment after two years. The total matches the owner's expectations, who decides to sell.

Step 3: The employees are informed and included in the sale process. There's no going back now!

Step 4: The purchaser commences due diligence (looking into the company in fine detail). They find a few things they aren't keen on. Actually, quite a few things. They reduce the initial amount to be paid, and make payments two and three dependent on certain conditions (warranties), such as clients staying.

Step 5: The owner is now worried that the amount they might receive will be less than originally expected. They consider dropping out of the deal, however the employees and certain key clients have already been told. Furthermore, the owner has already moved on emotionally.

Step 6: The deal is signed with many warranties and conditions.

The amount of money that a business owner ends up with in their bank account at the end of the purchase period is often much lower than the initial amount of money they were offered for their business. This is not generally reported – no one wants to admit that they were duped.

This can be an extremely damaging process, not least to the clients and employees of the company.

The obsession with growth

One damaging side effect of the obsession with value is an inevitable obsession with growth in value.

Generally speaking, if a person pays £1m for a £100k p.a. profits, they expect to see the share price grow. This means growing profits. This can be achieved many ways: increasing sales; acquiring other firms for economies of scale; reducing costs through efficiencies; reducing costs through redundancies and lowering quality. There are many ways to increase 'shareholder value', not all of them to the benefit of the customer, the employees – or, indeed, the planet.

An increase in the share price is not the same as a better business

I was once chatting with two commercial property investment consultants at a networking event. They boasted of some of the deals they had recently put together.

One had bought a large office for a client for many millions of pounds. It came with a generous amount of car parking. They had realised that the rules on the size of parking spaces had changed since the building had been built. After having bought the building, they restructured the car park by reducing the size of the spaces, and increased the numbers of cars that could be parked there by 20%. They then sold these additional spaces to the tenants.

They made a few other changes to the building of a similar nature, then sold the building on at a 10% profit after six months. By focusing only on capital growth, they had not actually improved the business at all – indeed, it could be argued that the tenants were worse off.

Recently, a huge global corporation decided to shut down a UK factory and move production to another country to save costs. The product in question is the sort of product that might get put into a basket of goods that typify Britain. The area in question is synonymous with the product, which has been located there for some 200 years.

The European CEO of the huge international company said that moving the factory was the "right thing to do for the business". What he actually meant, of course, was that it was the right thing to do for the shareholders. It may have added a few pence to the share price, but it cost hundreds of jobs directly and potentially thousands indirectly.

When a business is not owned by unconnected third parties concerned only with growing their share price, but by the people who work within the company, the perspective on such decisions changes.

From the owner's perspective: why not just keep the profits?

A common reaction from a business owner contemplating a sale structure where they get paid out of future profits is: why not just keep the business and therefore keep the profits? There are a number of answers to this:

- *All* business sales are effectively paid for out of future profits. This could be an earnout payment over a few years out of future profits, or all upfront from reserves which will be replaced by future profits. The whole reason someone buys a business is to buy the profits.

- Retaining the shares and therefore keeping the profits doesn't achieve the primary objective, which is to make the business eternal. Nor would it achieve the objective of the existing owners wanting to leave the business.

- Employees of a company owned by a shareholder no longer involved in the running of the business but who takes the profits are notoriously difficult to motivate.

- There can be significant tax advantages to receiving the profits through the sale of shares rather than dividends or salary.

Being paid out over a period of time from future profits does, however, mean de-risking the business – increasing the chances of the payments being made becomes paramount. Which means taking all the steps needed to make a business eternal!

BUSINESS STRUCTURES: DIRECT OWNERSHIP – SCHEMES

There are some schemes which enable succession planning by the gradual build up of direct ownership. Such schemes could include share options, whereby an individual is given the option to buy a share in the future but at a guaranteed price. These can motivate employees to improve the value of the business, without the employee taking any risk. Or, indeed, having any voting rights. The selling of such shares can also be on a predetermined date or event.

Certain share incentive plans give tax advantages to employees for buying shares on a monthly basis, enabling them to build up their shareholdings over time. Such schemes work for many employers. Which type of scheme might be right for your company is something on which you should take advice.

It is a feature of such schemes, however, that ownership tends to be minority – usually share schemes provide a small incentive to the employees, but are not intended to actually hand over control. They can be highly effective for motivating employees but do not necessarily provide the owner with an exit route.

Such schemes still rely on two fundamental principles:

- the shares are owned
- the shares have a value.

To repeat: in order to make a business eternal, it needs an ownership structure that doesn't lead employees to be focused on a sale. It means removing the idea that the shares have a value.

As long as the shares have a value, someone will want or need to sell them one day. Take away the focus on the possibility of a future sale means taking the focus away from the notion of value. When this happens, the approach to the business changes from increasing value with a view to a bumper payday to **long-term sustainable profit**. It leads to reduced risk and longer-term thinking.

One way of all but removing the possibility of the future sale of the business is for the business not to be owned by anyone, but the shares to be held for the benefit of the employees. An eternal business is therefore likely to mean indirect ownership.

INDIRECT OWNERSHIP

Indirect ownership of a business means that the shares are owned by a separate legal entity such as a trust fund. The primary advantage for a person looking to establish an eternal business is that the shares are not owned by individuals, but by a trust fund for their benefit. There are no issues with returning shares in the event of an employee leaving, and no obsession with value.

There are two main issues confronting an owner interested in moving their company to indirect ownership:

- which structure to move to

- how to get there.

The common terminology for a company that is owned by a trust fund for the benefit of its employees is that it is an 'employee-owned' business. First, then, let's look at what an employee-owned business looks like, and what the advantages are for the employees, owner and customers.

Then we'll look at how to move from a business that is owned and controlled by one or a few people to one that is employee-owned.

PART 2: THE EMPLOYEE-OWNED BUSINESS

The Employee Ownership Association (EOA) defines employee ownership as business that "are totally or significantly owned by their employees".

Another definition might be that **an employee-owned company is owned for the benefit of the employees.**

Employed-owned businesses that are not controlled by the employees are well-placed to last for a long time. However, a company that wants to be eternal needs, either at a given point or over a period of time, to give full control of the business to the employees. Once again, the notion of the four sides of the eternal pyramid relying on each other is relevant here. Without ultimate control of the business, employee engagement is unlikely to be maximised.

For this reason we will focus on companies in which the employees have a controlling interest. This is not to exclude companies that are on a path towards being fully employee-controlled – the principles of the eternal business will apply equally to such businesses.

OVERVIEW OF EMPLOYEE OWNERSHIP TRUSTS (EOT)

In the UK, an employee ownership trust (EOT) is a special type of trust that has been created to allow employees to participate in the ownership of a business. The EOT owns the shares of the business and the beneficiaries of the EOT are the employees.

Author's note: *For this section I am specifically assuming the use of an employee ownership trust (EOT). There are other forms of employee ownership model available, however the EOT is the one that has been created in the UK specifically for the purpose of employee ownership. The* *principles of the eternal pyramid are general, however, and apply equally to other forms of employee ownership.*

To reiterate the comments from the Introduction to this book, indirect ownership by way of a trust is not unique to the UK. Although the EOT is a UK innovation, which provides specific tax advantages, indirect ownership is also common in other countries such as the USA. You should seek legal advice on what structures are available where you live.

It is important to emphasise that the employees do not own the shares themselves. They do not need to buy in (and, of course, they are unable to sell out, with both the advantages and problems accompanying such a transaction). They *do* benefit from the profits, as beneficiaries of the trust, but do *not* actually own the shares.

This creates real empowerment for the employees as they have control over the business, and participate in the success (or otherwise) of the business, in the form of the profits.

Real empowerment

Earlier in the book we saw how The National Self Build and Renovation Centre moved to an employee-owned business during a period of difficult trading. Since then the company has thrived and staff morale and enthusiasm has increased manifold. All employees are involved in decision-making and committed to the business for the long haul.

Louise Jarmey is front-of-house manager, and comments: "We don't see ourselves as working *for*

The National Self Build and Renovation Centre: we *are* The National Self Build and Renovation Centre! Coming to work each morning is exciting, and we all feel the same passion for seeing the company thrive and are proud to be a part of its success."

This is how an employee ownership trust works:

- A trust is established by the company. The beneficiaries of the trust are the employees of the business (and can include dependants of deceased employees).

- The existing shareholders of the business then sell some or all of their shares to the trust.

- The shares are paid for by a deferred consideration – a debt is therefore created from the trust to the ex-owner.

- A proportion of the profits (as decided by the executive) from the business goes to the trust as the new shareholder.

- The trust uses these profits to repay the debt.

- Once the debt is repaid (and therefore the ex-owner has been bought out), more of the profits are available to be distributed among the employees.

Let us take an example where the owner sells 70% of their shares to the trust, retaining 30%. Such a structure is known as a **hybrid EOT,** as the company ends up with more than one shareholder.

Once the owner has been paid, the structure of the ownership, and direction of profits, would be as per the diagram below:

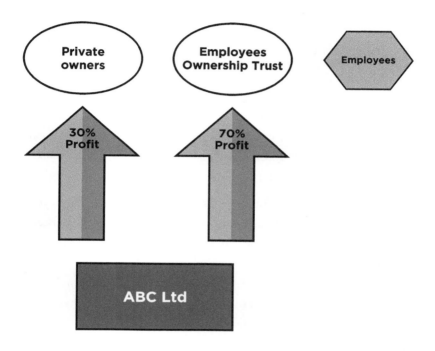

For tax reasons the profits may be distributed directly to the employees without actually being owned by the trust. Professional advice should be sought on this point.

Note that the amount of profits to be paid to the employees should be for the trustees to approve – who are representative of the employees! Other options would include reinvestment in the business, strengthening the balance sheet, acquisition or charitable donations.

Control of the company

The ownership of the business has now changed. The new owner (either in part or entirety) is the EOT. Note, however, that the trustees of the EOT do not *run* the business – the trust is the shareholder, not the manager.

As with any other business, the shareholders (the trust) appoints a board of directors to run the business on their behalf, in the same way that individual shareholders would. This could even be the same board as before. In this way we can see that the business can continue to run as before, nothing needs to change immediately within the business itself. It is only the *ownership* that is changing.

However, given that the business is now owned by the employees (via the EOT), if the board were to remain unchanged, perhaps including the previous owner, and the board were to continue to run the business as before, this is likely to lead to disquiet amongst the employees. A business that has moved to being employee-owned with no other changes is going to face significant challenges in becoming an eternal business.

When the moment comes that the business is sold to the trust for the benefit of the employees, the business should ideally be operating in accordance with a clearly defined sense of purpose (the flag); decision-making should already be devolved away from a select few; and employees should have clarity over their future to see how the profit-share will benefit them.

And so we find that we have travelled full circle. For this is the very reason why all four sides of the eternal pyramid need to be built before the final act of the sale of the shares to the EOT.

The trustees

The role of the trustees is the same as for any other independent shareholder of a business: to hold the board of directors to account for the performance of the business.

There is, however, a second role, that of representing the interests of the beneficiaries of the trust – the employees.

Given this dual role, the choice of the trustees is key. It is advisable that they should include *at least* one employee, to help ensure that the interests of the beneficiaries are represented. Other options for trustees might include a director to represent the board back to the trustees, and/or a retiring shareholder who is familiar with the business.

An independent trustee can also be a good idea, perhaps to bring in expertise otherwise unavailable, and to counter any possible conflict of interest held by other trustees. In addition, as someone unable to benefit from profits of the business, they can provide an opinion that is untainted and truly independent.

The terms of the trust are set at the outset, and therefore set by the existing shareholders. This gives the current owner the ability to determine certain key criteria. Without wishing to state the obvious, however, if these criteria were not generally in the best interests of the employees, it would be unlikely that the business would become eternal!

How are the profits distributed?

The profits of the business belong to the shareholders (after the board has made allowance for issues such as working capital and investment).

The beneficiaries of the trust are the employees. The profits therefore get distributed to the employees.

In what proportion the profits are paid to the employees is for the trustees to decide. Very often the trustees will consult the employees when deciding on the formula for the distribution of the profits.

There are, however, limitations on how the profits can be shared (this is to stop 'sham' EOTs being formed to give owners the tax advantages, but who then continue to pay themselves most of the ongoing profits).

A company owned by an employee ownership trust must distribute payments (which may in part be free of income tax) on a 'same terms' basis to employees. The payments may, however, take into account:

- eligibility criteria, such as only being able to participate 12 months after commencing employment

- length of service

- salary (pro rata, to take into account variable hours).

That's it! Note that individual or departmental performance is specifically NOT allowed to be one of the criteria.

That doesn't mean, of course, that the company can't have a bonus system that is based on performance. It simply means that the income-tax-free part of the distribution of the profits to employees cannot be based on performance.

A diligent and hard-working employee may consider it unfair that performance is not permitted as a criteria for profit-share. They may feel aggrieved that another employee who does not contribute in meetings and always goes home bang on time should get the same share of profits that they do.

There is an implication in such a complaint that this is an unfair situation, and that someone should do something about it. However, this is an employee-owned business. If another employee isn't performing, and yet will receive equal profits, *the other employees* should do something about it. That's what employee ownership is partly about – empowerment and taking responsibility.

Making a genuine contribution

Leading Lives is a social enterprise in the care sector. It came out of the NHS and an early decision was made for the company to be employee-owned. This was thought appropriate because their service was highly personalised – and the best way to personalise the service was for employees to be directly involved in decision-making.

Any employee is able to join the company's board, which is decided upon by 'members'. Any employee can become a member. Being a member is not compulsory – but most employees are members (78%), demonstrating the commitment of the employees to the business.

Members are co-owners in the business and have the opportunity to contribute. The high take-up of membership is testament to the efforts of the company to involve the employees in the business, and how much this is valued.

There is one other important feature of Leading Lives. It is a not-for-profit organisation. The engagement of the employees is not because they expect to get a share in the profits, but because they are able to make a genuine contribution to the success of the business.

The eternal business – removing the possibility of a sale

One of the attractions of indirect ownership is that it provides the ownership structure to create an eternal business. Whether the driving force behind this is to leave a legacy in the form of the business, or perhaps to retain a minority shareholding for an ongoing income, once at least 51% of the company is sold to the trust, control is handed over.

The idea of an eternal business is one that cannot be sold. Technically, however, this cannot actually be achieved. Under trust law it is not possible to dictate what the trustees are and are not allowed to do (the legal expression is that it is not permissible to 'fetter the trustees' discretion'). There may be circumstances where selling the shares is the right thing to do – for example, in the event of a legal claim against the company, or insolvency.

When we describe an eternal business as being one that cannot be sold, therefore, we really mean that it cannot be sold **without the express agreement of all stakeholders and interested parties**. If everyone agrees that selling the shares is the best thing to do, then it should not be (and is not) possible to prevent it.

Malign influences

The possibility of the business being sold, however, also means allowing the possibility of a malign influence gaining control of the trust and forcing a sale, against the wishes of the founder(s).

There are mechanisms that can be put in place which can make this eventuality extremely unlikely, if not completely impossible. These include:

- retaining a shareholding over 25% and writing into the articles that any sale must require 75% or more of shareholder agreement (this also allows for an ongoing income from profit)

- retaining a single share and writing into the articles that any sale must require 100% of shareholder agreement

- as trustees can only act unanimously, making one of the trustees an external trustee, i.e. not employed by the company.

Of course, the other course of action is to enact the other parts of this book! One of the drivers for the eternal pyramid model is to provide a place to work where employees would not *want* the business to be sold.

A final word on indirect ownership

Through indirect ownership, with the shares being owned by a trust, the business takes a significant step towards becoming an eternal business. The owner has a way out; profits will be shared with employees; the shares cannot be sold (to all intents and purposes).

Employee ownership is not for the faint-hearted, however. It is not just a transaction, it is a change to a different way of working. The Employee Ownership Association (**www.employeeownership. co.uk**) holds regular meetings and conferences full of people discussing issues such as how to identify and communicate the company vision, employee engagement, and collaborative decision-making.

In talking to employee-owned businesses, the majority of the issues that they have come up against *after* having become employee-owned have been covered somewhere within the eternal pyramid model.

PART 3: HOW TO GET THERE

So where do we now find ourselves?

The owner has decided to sell to a trust that they will establish. The employees have been informed and a plan has been created for the transition of control – for making the business eternal.

The company has gone through a period of introspection, including identifying the flag and ensuring it is applied and reflected throughout the business. Employees feel a connection with each other and a shared sense of purpose.

The employees have been brought into the decision-making structures of the business; the owner has successfully handed over control of the business.

Employees have understood that they are not going to have the opportunity (or be required) to find the money to buy shares in the business. Some were initially happy (as they had no intention or ability to buy shares), others less so.

Many employees, including all the leadership team, have their own personal financial plans providing a clear path to identifiable objectives, and clarity over their careers. Consequently, most of those less happy at not being able to buy shares have realised that the profit-share is a less risky alternative.

The owner decided on the trust ownership route some time ago. They then spent a few years getting the business in the right shape to be employee-owned. Now everything is in place. They are the least important person in the business

It's time to sell.

No big deal

If the principle of deciding first but actioning last has been followed fully, the act of selling to the trust should actually be rather uneventful. Everyone knows what is going to happen, the decisions have all been taken, it's pretty much just a question of the legal bods doing their thing.

Indeed, if there are any serious difficulties at this point, it might be a symptom of the fact that the pyramid is not yet fully built! And if the owner still has doubts or concerns, it might be that their own financial planning and plans for the future need a little more work.

Valuing the shares

The shares that are going to be sold need to be valued in order to decide how much the trust is going to pay the owner (who might now be called the vendor!). In order to demonstrate that this is a commercial transaction, the valuation must be independent. This is to ensure that an owner doesn't sell the business at an inflated price in order to benefit from any tax advantages.

The owner can, however, choose to sell the business for an amount lower than the independent valuation recommends. Indeed the owner could even choose to gift the shares to the trust, should they wish to do so.

A valuer is therefore appointed who will use standard criteria (such as profit levels and typical market ratios) to provide both parties with an independent valuation.

Establishing the trust

The company needs to set up the trust. This means the current owner gets to decide on a few important issues, such as the nature of the trustees, how frequently they meet, and so on.

As has already been mentioned, it is advisable that the current owner consults with the employees on such issues. The trustees are there to represent the interests of the beneficiaries of the trust, namely the employees. If the employees have the feeling that the trustees are not likely to represent their best interests, control will not be perceived to have been handed over, employees are unlikely to be engaged, and the eternal pyramid will collapse.

Advisers can be very helpful at this stage. Legal advisers are essential in setting up the trust anyway, but they (or business advisers who specialise or have experience in employee ownership) can provide an independent voice. In this way the employees can have questions answered, and seek reassurance that the arrangement is being established in everyone's best interests.

Employee reassurance

Employees are often sceptical of any changes made by the boss. A friend once asked me to look over some paperwork relating to a change to their company employee pension scheme. He was a senior member of the team but was not involved in the decision. He and several colleagues had a suspicion that the company was trying to worsen their conditions in an underhand way.

I looked at the paperwork and, in fact, the pension scheme was being improved by the change. Not only that, but the costs of making the change to the scheme were being met by the employer, resulting in very low charges to the scheme.

My friend was pleasantly surprised. Indeed, it opened his eyes to the fact that his immediate reaction had been negative, and led him to sit down with the owner of the company to discuss communication within the business.

Very often employees will assume that any changes to their benefits package or the structure of the business are going to adversely affect them. This 'them and us' mindset needs to have been largely overcome before the sale of the shares to the trust.

Funding the purchase

The newly established trust will not have the money to buy the shares. It does, however, have two ways of funding the purchase:

- From the future profits of the business.

- The trust may be able to borrow money to buy the shares. This is usually only for part of the purchase price, and is used if the vendor(s) wants an upfront payment.

The terms of the sale of the shares to the trust will include how much of the future profits will be used to finance the scheduled repayments of the purchase price, or repayment by the trust of any borrowings. For example, all the profits could be used to fund the purchase price and repay any debt as quickly as possible, thereby reducing the time before employees receive the profits. Alternatively, some of the profits could be distributed to staff with the remainder being used to fund the purchase prices or repay the debt over time.

A compromise will enable the owner to be repaid as quickly as possible without placing the company in any financial difficulty. In effect, there needs to be a carefully constructed balance to ensure that the owners get their money while ensuring the firm isn't put into trouble (which is, obviously, in no one's best interest – including the owner who is still owed money).

In some ways, the owner is negotiating with themselves when selling the shares to the trust. How the profits are split between funding the purchase price or repayment of the debt, and the employees, is up to the owner to decide when establishing the sale and purchase agreement. However, it is fair to say that if the employees are not consulted and a structure is put in place that they do not like, they will not stay. And that is unlikely to lead to the creation of an eternal business!

Sale and purchase agreement

The terms of the sale of the shares need to be covered in a sale and purchase agreement. Given that the payment for the business will come from profits generated out of a business that the vendor no longer controls, it is important to cover certain eventualities. The point of this book is to reduce the chance of such eventualities, and to give the business the best chance of being eternal, but there will always be unforeseen circumstances or events outside of the control of the business.

The sale and purchase agreement will include what happens if the company is unable to meet its liabilities to the vendor, and might also lay a template for how the company's profits are to be used during the payment period.

As with many legal documents, the sale and purchase agreement exists to provide clarity in case things go wrong. Other such documents may also be needed, for example a revised shareholders' agreement if the vendor is retaining a shareholding.

It should go without saying that paying for proper legal representation from a firm experienced with employee ownership trusts is critical when this stage of the transition has been reached.

Adversarial legal advice

It is the nature of law that where a negotiation takes place, one solicitor acts for one party, and another solicitor acts for the other. Each seeks the best outcome for their client, which so often leads to conflict.

In this instance, however, one party is the owner of the business, the other party is the trust – which is in the process of being established by the owner of the business. In order to prevent abuse of this situation, certain provisions are made, such as the need for an independent valuation.

There is also a natural mechanism – if the deal is skewed in favour of the vendor to the detriment of the employees, they will not be motivated to continue running the business profitably and generate the profits needed to make the payments!

It might, in such a situation, be expected that the employees take their own legal counsel. However, the employees do not have any say in the deal or the trust that is being established. The company itself is not changing, nor are their terms and conditions, it is the ownership that is changing, and this is not something employees are able to influence. It is good practice for employees to be kept informed of the changes, as with any other change of ownership, but unusual for them to seek their own advice.

Once the trust is up and running it may be that the trustees wish to take their own legal counsel. If they indicate that it is important for them to do so, any such request should be taken seriously by the board.

CONCLUSION

And so we reach the end of the journey. It's a strange time for the owner, getting to the point that you have been working towards for so many years. There is pride in seeing the business you worked so hard to establish stand on its own feet and declare that it no longer needs you. There may also be conflicting emotions over no longer being needed.

This is also the start of another journey – for the employees. By the time the sale to the trust takes place, the company should be running as if it were already employee-owned. No business can ever be considered 'finished', however. Employee-owned companies face their own unique challenges in their bid to become truly eternal.

In the final chapter, therefore, we'll look at what to do in order to successfully complete the journey to employee ownership, and see what we can learn from the experiences many companies have faced when they have become employee-owned.

Chapter 7

THE JOURNEY TO AN ETERNAL BUSINESS

INTRODUCTION

Moving to an eternal business is not a quick process.

Back in chapter 1 we looked at the challenges facing the business owner as they sought to do the right thing by their employees, their vision, and their own finances. We looked at the reasons why a business owner might consider making their business eternal.

Running a business is organic. Every day throws up fresh challenges. For many, that is part of the fun of running a business! In this book we have covered the four key aspects of giving a business the best chance of becoming eternal.

In this final chapter we'll recap and summarise the process of becoming an eternal business by looking at the steps to be taken. Timing is everything. As we go through the steps, we'll also hear about issues faced by companies who have already transitioned to being employee-owned.

The steps are:

Step 1: The owner decides if an eternal business is right for them.

Step 2: Involve senior employees.

Step 3: Owner and senior team develop the eternal strategic plan.

Step 4: Inform all employees.

Step 5: All employees get involved in turning the eternal strategic plan into the eternal action plan.

Step 6: The sale.

Step 7: Life in an eternal business.

It is key that these steps are followed in order. As we build the eternal pyramid we need to ensure the foundations are solid before we build upwards.

Managing expectations – how long will this process take?

If being eternal is at one end of a spectrum, at the opposite end is what we might refer to as the **personality business** – one dependent upon a dominating individual personality.

A personality business is likely to feature the following characteristics:

- one controlling shareholder
- the boss being the most important person in the business
- the vision living in the head of the boss
- clients always deal with the boss
- most employees clock in on time and leave on time
- some employees are frustrated because they'd like to get more involved with decisions and the direction of the business
- outsiders view the company as the boss's business.

The sort of language you might hear in a personality business might be comments from the boss such as, "The clients have always dealt with me, they simply won't speak with anyone else."

At the other end of the spectrum, as said, is the eternal business, with these characteristics:

- employee-owned
- no specific boss
- a clear flag in the ground to which all employees subscribe
- clients know and communicate with multiple employees
- employees willing to get in early or stay late when necessary
- most employees involved with decision-making
- outsiders view the company as a business.

As an estimate, it is likely to take **at least five years** to move from one end of the spectrum to the other.

Decide first, action last

Many businesses that have moved into employee ownership report that the issues they faced would have been easier to deal with if they had been addressed *before* the company became employee-owned. As one employee-owned company pointed out, decisions are subject to much greater scrutiny by employees when getting it wrong would be to their detriment.

In an ideal world, therefore, the company will have moved all the way along this timeline before the business is sold. Decide first, action last.

The owner is likely to have a very general idea of where the business might be on this timeline. This rough assessment is likely to inform their decision on the practicalities of making their business eternal.

Getting in shape before making the move

Jeremy Gadd of Jeremy Gadd Associates has been advising businesses as they transition to employee ownership for many years. He has seen a variety of different reasons for businesses choosing to become employee-owned, and understands the importance of getting the business in the right shape before making the move.

As he says: "In my experience a badly run business is unlikely to be saved by becoming employee-owned."

Now let's take a look at those steps in a bit more detail.

STEP 1: WHAT DOES THE FUTURE LOOK LIKE?

By the end of this step, the owner will know whether becoming an eternal business is right for them.

Before starting out on the path to becoming an eternal business, the owner needs to decide that this is indeed what they want. How much does the owner need to sell the business for (assuming the sale is by choice)? How does this compare with the likely independent valuation?

This in itself raises another question, which is what sort of life does the owner want once the business has been sold? How much will that cost? Will they continue to be involved in the business? Will they need an ongoing income? Will they sell all the business or just a controlling share?

This financial planning process may suggest a timescale. How long the process takes will therefore be dictated in part by the desire or need of the owner to exit the business. An assessment of the business will be helpful to determine how ready it is for employee ownership. This will provide the owner with a timescale to compare with that of their personal needs.

The owner may, at this point, wish to begin their own personal thoughts on finding the flag – setting out their own headline vision for the business.

Deciding to move towards eternal

Once you've told employees of your intention to become an employee-owned business, it is difficult to back out. Before doing so, therefore, the owner need an understanding of:

- their desired future

- their financial position

- the length of time it will take to become eternal.

These may well require expert assistance and will help the owner decide on the future they would like for their business.

It is important to note, however: if the journey towards employee ownership turns out not to be what you thought it would be, the steps you will have taken will still have made the business attractive for a more traditional sale to the management team or to a third party.

If this does come to pass, in the interests of credibility and trust it would be advisable to fully explain the reasons for *not* transitioning to employee ownership.

STEP 2: EXPLAIN THE PLAN TO SENIOR EMPLOYEES

By the end of this step the senior employees will be just as excited about the move to employee ownership as the owner.

Once the decision has been made to become an eternal business, the next step is to involve the senior employees.

The importance of getting the commitment of senior employees to becoming employee-owned will be self evident. There can often be a natural inclination among some employees towards a mistrust of the employer, however, and therefore getting employees onside is best done with care and at a pace that is right for them.

Some business owners, who felt they were doing a noble thing by selling to an EOT when they could have held on and kept the profits or sold to a large corporate for a higher price, reported frustration that their plans were treated with suspicion and hostility by some of their employees. Getting senior employees onside early means that there is someone other than the boss (who is perceived as potentially having vested interests) spreading the message of employee ownership across the business.

It is also possible that some senior employees may feel frustrated if they thought that they were going to be able to buy into the business in some way.

Using outside help to explain the concept to senior employees can also be a good idea to give independence to the message.

STEP 3: ASSESSMENT AND THE ETERNAL STRATEGIC PLAN

By the end of this step an outline plan will have been produced, plotting the issues to be considered on the journey to employee ownership, and a communications strategy for all employees will be ready to roll out.

Once the concept has been understood and accepted by the senior team, the next step is to jointly develop the original assessment of where the business sits on the timeline, perhaps using the eternal pyramid model as the guide.

The purpose of this assessment is to create an outline plan – it will naturally suggest gaps. However, a word of caution. It is tempting to begin suggesting and implementing specific changes, especially with an enthusiastic leadership team motivated by finally being allowed to help shape the future of the business.

It might be wise, though, not to take too many decisions or be too prescriptive at this point. If the business is to be employee-owned, decision-making needs to be devolved among *all* employees, not just a chosen few. The business will one day be owned by a trust for the benefit of all employees, so beware of taking action at this early stage.

Rather than working on specific changes to the business, the owner and senior employees should produce a strategic plan for how to become an eternal business. It should focus on the areas to be dealt with, but refrain from making too much comment on what changes might be necessary. This is the chance for the owner to show genuine commitment to handing over control.

This **eternal strategic plan** should include a communications strategy for how to get all employees onside; for example, how to consult and engage with employees so that everyone can contribute to the future shape of the business.

This eternal strategic plan should therefore take two parts: an overview of the needs of the business before it can become eternal; and a specific plan for how to involve all employees in the process.

STEP 4: START SPREADING THE NEWS

By the end of this step all employees will understand the concept of employee ownership and how it affects them.

Once the senior team are on board it is time to explain the plan for employee ownership to the rest of the employees; in other words to share the eternal strategic plan. It is important that everyone knows that the ultimate objective is employee ownership so that their input is appropriately targeted. People will also need time to get used to the idea of being business owners.

Meeting fellow pioneers

One method of getting employees used to what it means to be part of an employee-owned company – and to help the owner get used to the transition they need to go through – is to meet people who have trodden the path before them.

Through regional meetings, forums and their annual conference, the Employee Ownership Association (EOA) brings together employees and owners of businesses that are employee-owned; are in the process of becoming employee-owned; or are wondering if employee ownership is right for them.

I had been looking for the right ownership model for Ovation for some time. The day I first attended an EOA regional meeting was like being struck by lightning! After years of discussion around succession planning – all focused on concepts of value, sale and buyouts – I finally met people who understood me, who shared my values and objectives.

The employees of Ovation then attended subsequent meetings, where they met people who could share their experiences – and enthusiasm for – employee ownership. Through the EOA we found a community willing to share and help each other to make our own version of an employee-owned business.

STEP 5: THE ETERNAL ACTION PLAN

By the end of this (long) step all the employees will have been engaged in first producing then implementing a specific plan towards employee ownership. The company will be ready to become employee-owned.

Both owner and employees now need to be involved in turning the eternal strategic plan into an **eternal action plan**. Remember, one day this is going to be their business. The owner should be encouraging the employees to get involved as much as possible; otherwise, how can the owner step away? Hand over copies of *The Eternal Business*, then step back!

Remember the principle of the eternal pyramid, that all sides need to be built at a similar pace. As employees gain further understanding of what being an employee-owned business really means, so this will: change the way in which they disseminate the flag; inform the construction of decision-making; and suggest to many that they need clarity over their future and the role of the company in their lives.

And don't forget to give the owner clarity over their future within the business. Help them to be 'pulled not pushed'.

As the decision-making begins to be devolved, so employees begin to start taking control by getting involved in making real business decisions. This is a process that needs careful management. Let's take a moment to look at a few issues other companies have come across during this phase.

It's not a democracy

When employees are first involved in decision-making, some may overestimate the amount of influence they can have in the running of the business. By selling shares into the trust, only the ownership of the company has changed. It's important that changes to the *control* within the business reflect the new ownership, but they are by no means compulsory.

A number of employee-owned businesses reported this scenario of inflated expectations. It proved damaging as those employees became disillusioned with the process, with some disengaging completely.

The important distinction to draw is the difference between ownership and control. The company wants employees to be engaged, to contribute to decisions, but this doesn't mean they should expect to get their way every time. Companies who have successfully found a balance that works seem to have managed employee expectations at an early stage; helped everyone understand how the decision-making process works; and been clear on how much of an influence employees will really have.

Ultimately it is for the board to run the company, but with the employees able to contribute their ideas and opinions. At one employee-owned company, business-critical decisions are made by the board, all other decisions require contributions from the employees. The board prepares and presents the business plan, which is then voted on by the employees.

One employee reported that their company did not have clarity over who made which decisions. The employees thought they had a say, so when the board announced that they were opening a new office, without having consulted employees on the decision, the employees were unhappy and became disengaged.

Talking to each other differently

Partners at the John Lewis Partnership have various ways that they are able to put their views across. It is entirely possible that a person who works on the tills in Waitrose can, by being elected, challenge the Chairman of the company. That challenge will be treated with respect and answered accordingly.

The use of the term 'Partners' is important. Those elected to represent the views of their colleagues are not acting like a shop steward, representing workers against the bosses. In an employee-owned business, the employees are the bosses.

As board member David Jones puts it, being Partners does not change the need for debate amongst colleagues and with management, but it does mean you talk to each other differently.

Creating teams – personality profiling

Many firms reported that they faced issues in the early stages of devolving decision-making, when employees first came together to start making business decisions. The lines and boundaries of how people deal with each other change significantly – people might be put in a decision-making group with people several tiers their superior and asked to contribute on an even footing.

The dynamics can be very strange when you have spent several years looking to the boss for critical decisions, to then be asked by that very same boss for contributions to decisions.

As touched upon in chapter 4, a major step-change in teams making better decisions has been brought about by personality profiling (of which there are a number of proven models). All members of the team take the test, and the results are discussed (using outside facilitation at this stage was reported to be helpful). Despite the early cynicism of several members of some teams, the end result was that people understood each other better, and in particular how they reacted to conflict.

Some members of a team want to make quick decisions and move on, whereas others need time to consider all angles. Understanding how each member makes their own decisions results in a coming together to make better collective decisions.

STEP 6: THE MOMENT OF TRUTH

By the end of this step the company will be sold to the employee trust.

The business should be sold to the trust *only* when the business owner feels that the business is now running effectively without them – when they really are the least important in the business. The period between step 5 and step 6 could be several years.

Of course, achieving this moment is not always going to be possible, for a variety of reasons. Perhaps the business is struggling and employee ownership seems the only option for it to continue; maybe the owner has personal reasons for exiting the business quickly.

If step 6 does need to happen earlier than ideal, this does not change the importance of building the eternal pyramid. Taking time to ensure all the team fully understand the implications of employee ownership, and making sure the structures are in place for good decision-making, are if anything *more* important to follow diligently if the business has already been sold to a trust.

STEP 7: BEING EMPLOYEE-OWNED

There is no end to this step – that's the whole point!

No company is ever 'finished'. New challenges constantly present themselves – for many, that's the fun part of running a business!

Once the company has become employee-owned it will face its own challenges. Hopefully, however, it will be better placed to deal with them if it took the time to get into the right shape for an eternal business before making the big change.

The founder that hangs around too long

One of the principles of the eternal business is that the employees are making business decisions; that control has now truly transitioned from the old owner to the employees.

Once the shares have been sold to the trust, it is tempting for a founder to want to have ongoing input in the day-to-day running of the business. This is especially likely when the founder's payments are to be made out of future profits.

This can be a major mistake. Rather like the overbearing parent, if the founder does not allow employees to run the business in their own way, learning from their mistakes, it is unlikely that the employees will ever fully engage with the business.

This is not to say that the founder cannot have an ongoing role within the business, just that the role should be clearly and carefully defined. This can actually be a wonderful opportunity for the founder to get back to doing the things they enjoy. It should not involve looking over the shoulder of the employees and telling them that: "We don't do it that way here."

Having real clarity over the ongoing involvement of the founder will ensure everyone knows the boundaries and enable employees to feel they really are taking control.

The many lives of an eternal business

Being owned by a trust really does mean that a company can last forever. When Baxendale sold its manufacturing business in 2000, there was approximately £20m left in the shell of the company, and an employee trust which owned the shares.

That capital, combined with the ongoing clear purpose of the trust to promote the benefit of any company employees then and in the future, and an enduring commitment to employee ownership, meant that the business was able to reinvent itself.

It achieved this by relaunching as an investment firm, providing capital to other businesses who wanted to become employee-owned. It later added a consultancy business advising other companies on all aspects of employee ownership.

Baxendale has gone from a foundry to boiler maker to management consultancy; from employee numbers in the single figures up to hundreds, back down to single figures – and up again. If Baxendale had been owned by individuals, they might have given up, sold the business, and walked away. As it is owned by a trust, however, it really can be considered an eternal business.

CONCLUSION

Taking the above steps will shift control of the business from one that is dominated by one or a few individuals to one that is well-placed to last forever. To being an eternal business.

For the owner, the process will have:

- ensured the business was not sold to a third party who didn't understand it
- enabled the business to continue their vision – to provide a legacy
- provided their employees with a fulfilling future and the chance of financial security.

In addition, the business will provide for the owner:

- the release of capital
- an ongoing income (if some shares are retained)
- a sense of purpose (if an ongoing role is retained).

For the employees, the new eternal business will:

- provide access to profits in the future
- provide meaning and fulfilment to their employment.

A FINAL (PERSONAL) THOUGHT

I magine a world where all businesses are employee-owned. How would this affect the economy? How would this affect the planet?

At the time of writing, employee ownership is a fledgling idea. Only a tiny number (some 0.001%) of companies in the UK with between 10 and 250 employees are employee-owned. It is being talked about more and more in America. It is a sector that is, in my view, about to explode.

Employee-owned businesses still operate in a competitive market. The notion of the free market, which underpins the capitalist economic system, is not compromised by employee ownership.

What *does* change, however, is the distribution of wealth. Rather than a small number of people receiving the value of a business by selling out, the employees keep the business going and share in ongoing profits.

The dominant voice in the running of the business also changes, from a minority to the majority. Rather than being run with the primary motive of increasing the share price to benefit the few, the company focuses on long-term sustainable profit for the benefit of the many. Consequently those who also want to look up and consider the future of the planet have a chance for their voices to be heard.

One can foresee the growth of small businesses once again, and the reversal of the consolidation which occurs when big businesses hoover up small firms and deliver increased shareholder value by economies of scale and little else.

Where there is action, however, there must be reaction. Will this process also result in publicly-owned companies, starved of smaller businesses to buy out in order to increase their share price, losing value? Will the stock market – the place in which our personal investments and pension funds reside – become less attractive? Or will those large corporations find other ways to increase value?

Maybe the rise of employee ownership will change our very obsession with wealth and growth? Maybe the focus of society might change back from accumulation to wellbeing? Perhaps that's a debate for another day...

One thing I have learned from my own experience, and from talking to and working with other companies as they transition to employee ownership, is that there are good ideas, but no right answers. Employee-owned businesses are not like other businesses; they are exciting places to work, and they are almost always excited to share what they have learned – hence this book! I hope your own path to employee ownership and creating an eternal business is as fulfilling as my own has been.

APPENDIX – A ONE-PAGE FINANCIAL PLAN

ESSENTIALS

First you will need to have the following:

- emergency savings
- life and critical illness insurance
- a valid will in place.

CONSIDERATIONS

It is also sensible to consider:

- reducing your level of debt, focusing first on high-interest loans such as credit cards
- taking out income-protection insurance
- putting a lasting power of attorney in place.

OBJECTIVES

You have established the objectives in order of priority (perhaps with the help of a financial planner, or by working through the first few chapters of *The Financial Wellbeing Book*).

1. [*Insert name of objective...*] [*Insert timescale...*] [*Insert funds required...*]

2. [*Insert name of objective...*] [*Insert timescale...*] [*Insert funds required...*]

3. [*Insert name of objective...*] [*Insert timescale...*] [*Insert funds required...*]

CURRENT SITUATION

Think about your different expenses, the first being your basic needs, e.g. food, rent and utility bills. The second being leisure, things you can do without but would prefer not to miss – e.g. eating out, newspapers and holidays. The final being luxury: things you enjoy but aren't important to you, e.g. a new car.

- Basic expenses £ [*Enter expenses...*]
- Leisure expenses £ [*Enter expenses...*]
- Luxury expenses £ [*Enter expenses...*]

You are currently employed and after all deductions you earn:

- [*Insert income...*]

Once you have taken off your expenses you are left with the following amount available to save to meet your objectives:

- disposable income available for regular investment
- lump sum available for investment.

ACKNOWLEDGEMENTS AND THANKS

A big thanks to Phil Bray of The Yardstick Agency for his considerable contribution to part 4 of chapter 3 (on communication strategy).

An equally big thank-you to Cathy Monoghan of PES for her help with chapter 5.

Thanks to Paul Hardman of Gregg Latchams solicitors for suggesting I check out the Employee Ownership Association, which helped me find the final part of turning Ovation into an eternal business.

Ben Watson of TLT Solicitors and Robert Postlethwaite of Postlethwaites Solicitors Ltd provided their considerable legal expertise in the area of EOTs.

My profound thanks also to the following who read the manuscript and provided invaluable input:

- Jeremy Gadd of Jeremy Gadd Associates
- Phil Young
- Catrin MacDonnell
- Ovation employees, notably Chris Hindle, Elizabeth Thomas, Tom Morris
- Claire James of Pivotal Moment.
- Clive Waller of CWC Research

And finally, thank you to the Employee Ownership Association for their amazing enthusiasm in promoting the concept. **www.employeeownership.co.uk**

BIBLIOGRAPHY AND REFERENCES

It would surely be remiss of me not to start the bibliography with my own book, *The Financial Wellbeing Book*. All proceeds go to the Penny Brohn UK cancer charity. The book will help anyone to work out a financial plan of their own – and it will be a plan based around what makes you happier not just wealthier. You might also check out *The Financial Wellbeing Podcast* (**www.financialwell-being.co.uk/podcasts**).

For organisational structures and collaborative decision-making, read *Reinventing Organizations* by Frederic Laloux.

For an effective communication strategy, try Bryony Thomas's brilliant *Watertight Marketing* book.

The Antidote by Oliver Burkeman provides a very different approach to issues such as goals. It's a great book for getting people to think differently – such as employees who need to think like business owners.

For motivating and rewarding employees, read *Drive* by Daniel H. Pink.

Traction by Gino Wickman has a lot to say on career plans and motivating employees.

For more on why employees leave, see the following links compiled by Cathy Monoghan of PES:

www.investorsinpeople.com/sites/default/files/IIP%20 Job%20Exodus%20Trends%20-%202017%20employee%20 sentiment%20poll.pdf

hbr.org/2016/09/why-people-quit-their-jobs

www2.cipd.co.uk/pm/peoplemanagement/b/weblog/archive/2017/05/19/one-in-five-uk-employees-have-resigned-over-a-terrible-boss.aspx

realbusiness.co.uk/hr-and-management/2016/01/05/5-key-reasons-why-a-third-of-uk-workers-want-new-jobs-in-2016

For more on management buyouts, see:

www.thembogroup.com/management_buyouts/management_buyouts_biggest_mistakes.html

news.bbc.co.uk/1/hi/business/4201229.stm